W9-CHK-728

The Earth Is the Lord's and All Those Who Live in It

Psalm 24:1

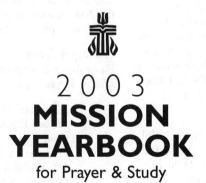

2 0 0 3
MISSION
YEARBOOK
for Prayer & Study

The Presbyterian Church (U.S.A.)'s *Mission Yearbook for Prayer & Study* is published by Witherspoon Press and produced by the Mission Interpretation and Promotion program team of Congregational Ministries Publishing, Congregational Ministries Division, a ministry of the General Assembly Council.

Lectionary

The lectionary is from the Presbyterian Church (U.S.A.)'s *Book of Common Worship*. The text for Sundays and festivals is originally from the *Revised Common Lectionary*, prepared by the Consultation on Common Texts. The daily lectionary in the *Book of Common Worship* is taken from the *Book of Common Prayer*, with revisions that were made for inclusion in the *Lutheran Book of Worship*. Psalm readings are sometimes repeated from week to week to help the reader absorb the words into memory.

Abbreviations

On the Lord's Day pages, abbreviations identify where hymn selections can be found—PH: *The Presbyterian Hymnal;* WB: *The Worshipbook*; HB: *The Hymnbook*; PPCS: *The Psalter: Psalms and Canticles for Singing*; and PCW: *Psalter for Christian Worship*. In the daily prayer lists, abbreviations are used to identify the areas in which General Assembly staff work—BOP: Board of Pensions; CMD: Congregational Ministries Division; EDO: Executive Director's Office of the General Assembly Council; DEDO: Deputy Executive Director's Office; FDN: Presbyterian Church (U.S.A.) Foundation; MSS: Mission Support Services; NMD: National Ministries Division; OGA: Office of the General Assembly; PAM: Presbyterian Association of Musicians; PILP: Presbyterian Investment and Loan Program; PPC: Presbyterian Publishing Corporation; PW: Presbyterian Women; WMD: Worldwide Ministries Division. (Note: General Assembly staff in prayer lists appears in alphabetical order.)

Cover Art

The image on the front cover is a watercolor painting by Nabil Anani, a member of the Palestinian Artists League. The central theme of the image shows the olive tree as symbolic of life in the rhythm of love and hope, as it endures for centuries and in very harsh conditions. Used with permission of the artist. All rights reserved.

Cover and Color Insert Section

The cover was designed by Mark Thomson. The color insert was designed by Patrick Hugg.

Photographs

Credits for photographs are listed on the pages where the photos appear.

Scripture

Unless otherwise noted, Scripture quotations are from the New Revised Standard Version of the Bible and are copyrighted ©1989 by the Division of Christian Education of the National Council of the Churches of Christ in the U.S.A. and are used by permission.

Order Information

Additional copies of the *Mission Yearbook* and the color insert, *The Creator, The Creation, and "Us,"* may be ordered (while supplies last) from:

Presbyterian Distribution Service
Presbyterian Church (U.S.A.)
100 Witherspoon Street
Louisville, KY 40202–1396
Telephone: (800) 524-2612

The *2003 Mission Yearbook* cost is $8.50 each or $7.50 each for 10 or more copies to the same address. PDS 70-612-03-450. The color insert, **The Creator, The Creation, and "Us,"** cost is $2.00 each; $9.00 for 5 copies; and $15.00 for 10. PDS 70-612-03-449. Please use the order card in the *2003 Mission Yearbook for Prayer & Study* to order the 2004 edition in advance of publication. To guarantee availability, please order before August 1, 2003.

Correspondence

Please direct correspondence (other than orders) about the *Mission Yearbook* to:

Managing Editor
Mission Yearbook for Prayer & Study
Congregational Ministries Publishing
Presbyterian Church (U.S.A.)
100 Witherspoon Street, Room 1418
Louisville, KY 40202–1396

Visit the *Mission Yearbook for Prayer & Study* Web site at http://www.pcusa.org/pcusa/cmd/mip/intro.html, or order the *Mission Yearbook* online in the Presbyterian Marketplace at www.pcusa.org/marketplace.

TABLE OF CONTENTS

MINUTE FOR MISSION INDEX

APPENDICES INDEX

Acknowledgments

The *Mission Yearbook* editorial team consists of Sharon K. Youngs, editor; Deborah Bowker Haines, managing editor and associate editor for domestic copy; Billie Healy, associate editor for international copy; Nancy Goodhue and Susan Salsburg, copy editors. The publisher for CMP is Sandra Moak Sorem. The *Mission Yearbook* was formatted by staff members Mark Thomson and Sherry Young. Staff members Margaret Hall Boone, Cecilia Amorocho Hickerson, Teresa Mader, Maureen O'Connor, and Lily Osuamkpe assisted the editorial team.

Hymn selections are by Guy S. Younce, director of music, Central Presbyterian Church, Louisville, Kentucky. Daily Scripture references were selected by the Rev. Lynn Williamson, First Presbyterian Church, Shelbyville, Kentucky. A suggested Outline for Daily Prayer was prepared by the Rev. Sharon K. Youngs.

We are also very grateful for the writings of Walter Brueggemann, William Marcellus McPheeters Professor of Old Testament, Columbia Theological Seminary, Decatur, Georgia, found in the color insert section.

Using the Daily and Sunday Lectionary

There are two lectionaries (cycles of readings) that are used by Presbyterians. One is the weekly lectionary. It is divided into years A, B, and C. From this cycle of readings many Presbyterians throughout the world determine the scriptural texts that will be read in corporate worship on Sundays. The other lectionary is offered for daily use and is divided into a two-year cycle. This series of readings is intended for use in daily corporate or individual worship. Both lectionaries are listed on Lord's Day pages in this edition of the *Mission Yearbook*. This enables those who wish to read the Lord's Day lections to do so, and those who wish to maintain an unbroken cycle of daily readings to honor that tradition. Hymns from *The Presbyterian Hymnal* (PH), *The Worshipbook* (WB), and *The Hymnbook* (HB) accompany the Sunday lectionary readings. *The Psalter: Psalms and Canticles for Singing* (PPCS) and the *Psalter for Christian Worship* (PCW) are also provided where appropriate.

Demographics

Information for country demographics was taken from *The World Factbook 2001*, published by the Central Intelligence Agency. Total area is the sum of all land and water areas delimited by international boundaries and/or coastlines. The GDP (gross domestic product) per capita is the value of all final goods and services produced within a nation in a given year per person. As a point of reference, demographic information on the United States is provided in the following box.

> **United States Total Area:** 3,535,000 sq. mi. (about three-tenths the size of Africa). **Population:** 278,058,881. **Languages:** English and Spanish. **GDP Per Capita:** $36,200. **Literacy:** 97%. **Religions:** Protestant, Roman Catholic, Jewish, other, none. **Life Expectancy:** 77.26 years. **Human Development Index Rank:** 6.

Human Development Index Rank

The Human Development Index (HDI), developed by the United Nations Development Programme, is a composite index of achievements in three fundamental human dimensions—a long and healthy life, knowledge, and a decent standard of living. Three variables have been chosen to represent these three dimensions—life expectancy, educational attainment, and income. The demographic information included on *Mission Yearbook* pages for international countries includes a ranking of countries by their Human Development Index values. The HDI rank for the United States is 6. The country with the highest HDI rank is Norway.

(From *Human Development Report 2001.* Copyright © 2001 by the United Nations Development Programme. Used by permission of Oxford University Press, Inc.)

Mission Personnel

Throughout this book you will find PC(USA) mission personnel, national and international, referred to in a number of ways. Both mission co-workers and mission specialists are fully compensated full-time international mission service workers appointed in response to an invitation by overseas ecumenical partner churches or institutions. Mission Volunteers International and Mission Volunteers U.S.A. are mission workers receiving a subsistence-living stipend and/or room and board for service of several weeks to two years. They may also raise a portion of the financial support for their term of service. Only volunteers serving for a year or longer are listed in the *Mission Yearbook*.

Learn more about becoming a part of the church's mission through service: for international service, call (888) 728-7228, ext. 2530 or visit www.pcusa.org.msr; for national service, call (888) 728-7228, ext. 5280 or visit www.pcusa.org/nvo.

2003 Children's Mission Yearbook for Prayer & Study

2003 marks the first edition of the *Children's Mission Yearbook for Prayer & Study*. This new resource is a personal devotional guide for third through fifth graders. As children work their way through the resource, they will be asked on occasion to find different items in the *Mission Yearbook*. For more information on this new resource, contact the managing editor of the *Mission Yearbook*.

The *Mission Yearbook for Prayer & Study* is widely used in daily prayer in homes and churches, at meetings, and in other settings. The outline suggested here offers a framework for daily prayer, using Scripture readings from the daily lectionary and passages from the *Yearbook*. In this way Presbyterians all over the world can be joined in prayer as brothers and sisters united in a common calling—the proclamation of the realm of God.

Opening Sentences (Ps. 92:1–2)

It is good to give thanks to the Lord,
to sing praises to your name, O Most High;
to declare your steadfast love in the morning,
and your faithfulness by night.

Hymn or Psalm

(Sing a hymn that is suitable for the day's lectionary passages, or use a psalm from the day's readings.)

Prayer for Illumination

Our understanding of your Word comes from you, O God. Open our ears, minds, and hearts to hear what you have to say to us. Help us upon hearing to understand, and upon understanding, to act; in Jesus' name.

Scripture Readings

Please refer to the lectionary passages for the day.

Prayers of Thanksgiving and Intercession

Give thanks for God's abundant gifts to us. Pray for the church and the needs of God's people in every part of the world, especially those called to mind today in the Mission Yearbook. *Conclude with the following prayer:*

Gracious Creator, once we were not a people; now we are your people. As you did in the beginning, move your Spirit over and among us, bringing harmony and order once again to your world and its inhabitants. We pray in the name of Jesus Christ, who showed us how to be in right relationship with you, and who taught the disciples when praying to say:
The Lord's Prayer

Dismissal (Matt. 7:12)

In everything do to others as you would have them do to you; for this is the law and the prophets.
Amen.
Bless the Lord.
The Lord's name be praised.

I invite you to join me on a mission trip around the world. The trip will take one year. The ministry we undertake will be a ministry of prayer. Our guide—the *Mission Yearbook for Prayer & Study*.

The *Mission Yearbook* does not annotate Presbyterian Church (U.S.A.) mission programs in a logical or institutional way (though one can find our polity and structure reflected in the arrangement of the content in the book). Rather, the book tells stories of how the Holy Spirit has worked through the life of our church as an institution, through partners in mission, and through many of our individual members. This year the book includes stories provided by more than 350 people.

Every summer for several years I have had the privilege of reading the *Mission Yearbook* straight through like a novel before it goes to print. This resource is not a novel intended for that sort of reading, but such a reading is powerful—even awe inspiring—as it reveals something of the scope and impact of mission and ministry made possible by efforts of the Presbyterian Church (U.S.A.).

Each *Yearbook* focuses on the church's mission from a particular theme. The 2003 theme is about restoration. Walter Brueggemann's essay, *The Creator, the Creation, and "Us,"* found in the color section, offers a thoughtful, theological understanding of what it means to say "the earth is the LORD's and all . . . those who live in it."

In monumental ways as well as simple ones, Presbyterians are at work in God's world. Whether called in this place or into many places, our lives bear witness to the living Christ. We respond not as

> *The book tells stories of how the Holy Spirit has worked through the life of our church as an institution, through partners in mission, and through many of our individual members.*

privileged, Western people sharing generously with others, but as some among all of God's children who share in the bounty of creation and who are called to serve Christ, to learn from one another, and to love our neighbors as ourselves.

—*Elder Sandra Moak Sorem, publisher,*
Congregational Ministries Publishing

Prayer

Holy Living God, bless our efforts to be faithful in all the places where we live and work. May prayers of gratitude flow unendingly for the blessings of life, for the earth itself, and for all those who dwell in it. May our spirits reflect your love and our actions prove our respect for all who share your bountiful world. We pray in Jesus' name. Amen.

How to Use the Prayer Lists

In this 111th year of the publication of the *Mission Yearbook for Prayer & Study*, readers are invited to join in prayer for the many people and ministries of the Presbyterian Church (U.S.A.).

Included in the prayer lists are synod and presbytery staff, General Assembly entity staff, General Assembly Council members, mission personnel, mission volunteers, and partner churches and organizations.

- Mission personnel and volunteers are listed on the page featuring the country or presbytery where they are working.
- General Assembly staff are listed alphabetically. Abbreviations following staff names identify the area in which they work:

BOP: Board of Pensions
CMD: Congregational Ministries Division
EDO: Executive Director's Office of the General Assembly Council
DEDO: Deputy Executive Director's Office of the General Assembly Council
FDN: Presbyterian Church (U.S.A.) Foundation
MSS: Mission Support Services
NMD: National Ministries Division
OGA: Office of the General Assembly
PAM: Presbyterian Association of Musicians
PILP: Presbyterian Investment and Loan Program
PPC: Presbyterian Publishing Corporation
PW: Presbyterian Women
WMD: Worldwide Ministries Division

- General Assembly Council (GAC) members are listed by presbytery.

A Message from the Moderator

Early in the Acts of the Apostles, Jesus said to the disciples, "But you will receive power when the Holy Spirit has come upon you; and you will be my witnesses in Jerusalem, in all Judea and Samaria, and to the ends of the earth" (Acts 1:8). The *Mission Yearbook for Prayer & Study* is like the Book of Acts in that it helps discover the mighty acts of God through the ministry and mission of the Presbyterian Church (U.S.A.). Jerusalem represents the mission work in our homes, congregations, and communities; Judea represents the mission work done through our presbyteries; Samaria represents the mission work done through our synods; the ends of the earth represent the mission work done through the General Assembly nationally and globally. The *Mission Yearbook* is the best educational tool for Bible study, prayer, and learning about the mission of the PC(USA). For this reason, I give each session member, staff member, and Sunday school class a copy.

The 2003 theme centers on the power of the psalmist's vision and concept that not only human beings, animals, and all living things belong to God, but also the earth—all of creation. God is calling us in the beginning of the twenty-first century not only to focus on restoring right relationship with our Creator through Jesus Christ: we need also to focus on restoring our relationship with the earth, remembering that the earth belongs to God.

As your moderator I want to thank God for our country. On January 29, 1966, I arrived in Lakeland, Florida, from Palestine with one suitcase, an Arabic Bible, and an English-Arabic dictionary to study. On June 15, 2002, I was elected your moderator. This can only happen in the church of Jesus Christ, only in the Presbyterian Church (U.S.A.), and only in the United States of America.

May this be a year of spiritual renewal in our lives and churches. May we experience unity amid our diversity; may our focus stay strong on local and global mission; and may we continue to do justice, love mercy, and walk humbly before our God. Salaam, Shalom, Peace!

—Rev. Fahed Labeeb Abu-Akel, moderator,
214th General Assembly, Presbyterian Church (U.S.A.)

THE SYNOD OF ALASKA-NORTHWEST

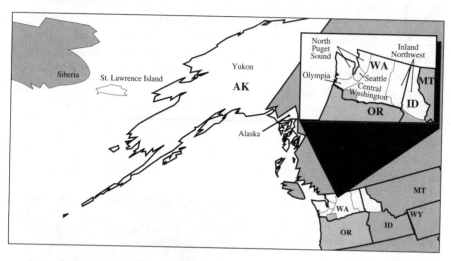

Creator of mountains, of glaciers and streams,
Great Splasher of fountains and Dreamer of dreams,
We gather in wonder and praise for Your grace.
Responding, we ponder our work in this place.

This first verse of "Creator of Mountains," written by Jane Parker Huber for the Synod of Alaska-Northwest, expresses wonderfully our call to ministry in the Pacific Northwest. Our synod not only covers a huge geographical area, 638,000 square miles, but is also diverse in cultures and rich in resources both human and physical. These resources include 273 congregations and 61,294 members in 7 presbyteries who seek daily to be faithful for the gift of grace given to them by the Creator.

A synod group, Presbyterian Earthkeepers, gathers yearly for biblical and theological study, for support and idea exchange, and to discover ways in the Spirit that they can bear witness to Ps. 24:1. This witness is surrounded by tension and anxiety as we try to live a balance between economic growth and protection of the environment. Pray that as "we gather in wonder and praise" our witness will indeed be given in concrete ways, proclaiming that "the earth *is* the LORD's and *all . . .* those who live in it."

Scripture

Make a joyful noise to the LORD, all the earth; break forth into joyous song and sing praises (Ps. 98:4).

Let Us Join in Prayer for:

Synod Staff
Rev. Dr. Douglas Kelly, synod executive
Rev. Gordon Cramer, stated clerk
Rev. Robert McClure, associate synod executive, stewardship and communication
Dean Mielke, director, financial services
Megan Lee, loan processor and accounting clerk
Marnie DelCarmen, administrative assistant, stewardship and communication
Elder Chris DeKay, administrative assistant, executive services
Elder Alma-jean Marion, synod moderator
Marty Warr, accountant, registrar

PC(USA) General Assembly Staff
Susan Abraham, WMD
Thomas Abraham, MSS
Rev. George Adams, BOP

Daily Lectionary

Ps. 8, 98, 99, 147:1-11
Gen. 17:1-12a, 15-16
Col. 2:6-12; John 16:23b-30

THE PRESBYTERY OF ALASKA

Let Us Join in Prayer for:

Presbytery Staff
Rev. Jay Olson, general presbyter
Elder Gail Coenraad,
administrative assistant
Elder Guy Warren, stated clerk

Mission Volunteers in the U.S.A.
Sheldon Jackson College, Alaska: **Jack
Ozment, Judith Ozment, James Watts,
Joann Watts, Elaine Zingg, Otto Zingg**

PC(USA) General Assembly Staff
Frances Adderley, BOP
Michael Agamemnonos, MSS
Rona Agnew, BOP

Nestled in a rain forest with rugged terrain and islands, the Presbytery of Alaska extends from the northern Tlingit village of Yakutat to Metlakatla, a Tsimshian village and the only reservation in the state. Although travel and transporting resources to support leaders and congregations continue to be very expensive, the Presbytery of Alaska is seeking exciting and creative ways to fulfill its mission and ministry.

The majority of congregations are small and isolated. For instance, Pelican, a small fishing community, is a mission preaching point. The Rev. Janice Stamper went to Pelican for two weeks to preach and administer the sacraments. She stayed to perform a wedding and was weathered in for a few days. She then traveled to Hydaburg on Prince of Wales Island to share leadership there with the Haida elders while they were without a pastor. The elders determined that they would meet together to pray for their community, the church, and the world.

Commissioned lay pastor Greg Howald is serving the church at Hoonah on Chichagof Island. The Hoonah Presbyterian Church is growing and now has its own Christian radio station. Leadership development is a mission priority, and the commissioned lay pastor program is vital to isolated communities.

The presbytery met together at Rainbow Glacier Camp in Haines, Alaska.

Christian inclusiveness is also a priority for the presbytery, so training elders includes intercultural, peacemaking, and justice issues. The diversity of cultures and peoples is being celebrated in new ways as the presbytery rejoices for God's faithful presence among Alaska's peoples.

Sheldon Jackson College in Sitka has a covenantal relationship with the PC(USA). The college is meeting with success in its transformation and has hired Dr. Carlyle Haaland as its president.

The Presbytery of Alaska has 15 congregations, 1 preaching point, and 1,320 members.

Daily Lectionary

Ps. 9, 29, 48, 147:12-20
Gen. 12:1-7
Heb. 11:1-12; John 6:35-42, 48-51

Scripture
Jesus said to them, "I am the bread of life. Whoever comes to me will never be hungry, and whoever believes in me will never be thirsty" (John 6:35).

THE PRESBYTERY OF CENTRAL WASHINGTON

The Presbytery of Central Washington seeks your prayers of joy and encouragement for the fellowship of believers brought together by the Westminster and First Presbyterian Churches of Yakima. Eight years ago the two churches joined together to provide leadership for the growing Hispanic population in the Yakima Valley. The Rev. Jorge Lopez, former moderator of the Presbyterian Church in Mexico, came to Yakima and started Bible studies, worship services, and youth ministries. Under his leadership for three years a nucleus of a congregation was brought together. The congregation of over eighty people currently worships at Yakima First Presbyterian Church.

Pastor Gustavo Carvajal (second from left) serves the Hispanic fellowship, which worships in a combined service of English and Spanish.

At the February 2002 Stated Meeting of the Presbytery of Central Washington, Gustavo Carvajal was approved to be a commissioned lay pastor to the Hispanic fellowship. Gustavo came to the United States from Colombia and is enrolled as a seminary student working toward ordination.

The Hispanic fellowship and the sponsoring churches are deliberate in planning combined worship services. For example, on Ash Wednesday in 2002 the Hispanic congregation and the congregation of Yakima First Presbyterian worshiped together in a combined service in English and Spanish. Worshipers came forward as an act of confession, writing their sins on paper before the cross. Those sheets of paper were burned to create the ashes for the service.

Pastor Gustavo and his wife, Katrina Carvajal, are thrilled with the outpouring of God's Spirit, which brings spiritual growth and the breaking down of racial barriers to the Yakima Valley. The presbytery hopes to see this model duplicated throughout its valleys.

The Presbytery of Central Washington serves 44 churches and 7,639 members.

Scripture

I am the gate for the sheep. . . . Whoever enters by me will be saved, and will come in and go out and find pasture (John 10:7, 9).

Let Us Join in Prayer for:

Elder Frances D. Irwin, member, GAC

Presbytery Staff
Rev. G. David Lambertson, executive presbyter
Debbie Dawson, administrative assistant
Rev. Muriel Brown, stated clerk

PC(USA) General Assembly Staff
April Aguillard, OGA
Yvonne Aiken, NMD
Elder Douglas Aitken, FDN

Daily Lectionary

Ps. 15, 107, 111, 148
Gen. 28:10-22
Heb. 11:13-22; John 10:7-17

Let Us Join in Prayer for:

Presbytery Staff
Rev. Richard Melin, executive presbyter
Joyce Bippes, administrative assistant
David Hamilton, stated clerk
Bob Bangerter, treasurer
Patsy Soliday, recording clerk
Sandy Riebe, financial administrator

PC(USA) General Assembly Staff
Rev. Antonio Aja, WMD
Elder Loyda Aja, OGA
Gail Alexander, NMD

THE PRESBYTERY OF INLAND NORTHWEST *Idaho, Washington*

The Presbytery of Inland Northwest in eastern Washington and northern Idaho is comprised of 50 congregations and 9,360 members. Half of the congregations have fewer than 100 and three-quarters have fewer than 200 members. The presbytery celebrates the diversity of the topography, communities, and cultures it comprises.

In a variety of ways throughout the presbytery congregations are working to be good and faithful stewards of what God has created. While not all practices are likely to make headlines, they are practical, grassroots attempts to be thoughtful and effective stewards.

One congregation makes space available in its parking lot for city recycling bins. Several congregations make provision for recycling their Sunday bulletins and other paper. In many congregations stickers remind parishioners to turn out the lights when leaving a room that's not in use. The presbytery shares information on the ENERGY STAR program with all congregations.

> *The issues of stewardship of natural resources and meeting community needs make for spirited debate and intense concern.*

In this region as elsewhere across the country, the issues of stewardship of natural resources and meeting community needs make for spirited debate and intense concern. For example, Presbyterians are among those on both sides of the issue concerning the spawning habits of salmon and the hydroelectric dams on the lower Snake River that provide transportation for farm products and water for the tourism and recreation bases of local economies.

Pray that we all may be good and faithful stewards.

Daily Lectionary

Ps. 20, 93, 97, 149
Exod. 3:1-15
Heb. 11:23-31; John 14:6-14

Scripture

God said to Moses, "I AM WHO I AM." He said further, "Thus you shall say to the Israelites, 'I AM has sent me to you'" (Exod. 3:14).

THE LORD'S DAY

MINUTE FOR MISSION
DAY OF PRAYER FOR THOSE PERSECUTED
AND MARTYRED FOR THEIR FAITH

Sunday Lectionary and Hymns

Jer. 31:7–14
PH 445

Ps. 147:12–20
Now Praise the Lord
PH 255; PPCS 154

Eph. 1:3–14
Christ, You Are the Fullness
PH 346

John 1:(1–9) 10–18
Born in the Night, Mary's Child
PH 30

The festivities of the Christmas season are winding down. As Christians in the United States we celebrate Advent and Christmas without hesitation or fear. We boldly proclaim the good news that Jesus Christ has come, Emmanuel, God is with us! We display our Nativity scenes, sing Christmas carols in our neighborhoods, and attend Christmas pageants, community presentations of Handel's *Messiah*, and special worship services. We are fortunate to live in a country that upholds the value and importance of freedom of religion and belief. We know, however, that this is not the case for many around the world who suffer, have been persecuted, and have even died because they have chosen to express their faith in countries where religious plurality is not accepted and is in some cases illegal.

As Presbyterians richly blessed with the freedom to express our faith without constraints, we set aside this day, the second Sunday after Christmas, to commemorate a Day of Prayer for Those Persecuted and Martyred for Their Faith. On this day we are asked to pray for all people who experience religious persecution around the world. We acknowledge in corporate worship and in our private reflections that the basic human right to practice the faith of one's own choice is not allowed in many parts of the world.

This is also a time when we can put our faith into action on behalf of those who are oppressed because of their religious conviction. We can support and encourage our worldwide ecumenical partnerships that have done much to build bridges of understanding and tolerance. We can also support efforts by the United Nations as it works to ensure the human rights of people, including freedom of religion. Our witness for justice, empowered by God through the Holy Spirit, will turn their mourning into joy.

—Elder Sara P. Lisherness, coordinator,
Presbyterian Peacemaking Program

Prayer
Gracious God, we give you thanks for the many blessings you have bestowed upon us and ask that your comfort be felt by those suffering religious persecution. In grateful obedience to you, may we use our voice to advocate freedom, justice, and the right to live faithfully for all people in every corner of the world. We ask this in the name of Jesus Christ. Amen.

Daily Lectionary
Ps. 96, 99, 110, 150
Josh. 1:1-9
Heb. 11:32–12:2; John 15:1-16

Let Us Join in Prayer for:

PC(USA) General Assembly Staff
Deeanna Alford, DEDO
Denise Allen, MSS
Ralph Allen, FDN
Mark Amstutz, BOP

EPIPHANY

MINUTE FOR MISSION

As a consultant to a philanthropy, I spent a week ushering foundation officials around Port-au-Prince, Haiti. The Duvalier dictatorship was still in power. My employers were reviewing their moratorium on grant making in Haiti. Against my advice, we stayed at a famous hotel. From that highly visible location, we visited the embassy, a human rights leader, and a bishop, and generally failed to keep a low profile. The wealthy trustee under my care noticed we were being followed. We learned that our driver had been coerced into sharing our itinerary.

Rose

photo by Marian McClure

When I arrived in northern Haiti to arrange the visit's second week, the military post official asked, "Where will you stay?" Unprepared for this question, I gave the address of my friend Rose. Rose, who supported her relatives by cooking for a Catholic priest in a remote mountain parish. Rose, who lived in one room and had a heart condition she could not afford to treat. Rose, who had helped me during my year of research and who was now vulnerable because of my connections to wealth and power.

Was this how the Wise Men felt when they arrived at Jesus' manger? Could they have refused Herod's hospitality, dodged his questions? Had their comfort in elite circles blinded them to how they were making it easier for the haves to hurt the have-nots?

They never came for Rose; no one wept for this one of "Rachel's children" on my account. But like the Wise Men, I had an epiphany: from then on I would always try to travel "by another road."

—*Rev. Dr. Marian McClure, director, Worldwide Ministries Division*

Daily Lectionary

Ps. 67, 72, 100, 145
Isa. 52:7-10
Rev. 21:22-27; Matt. 12:14-21

Prayer
God of the star-lit path, help us to know when a fork in the road asks whether we will choose on behalf of the more vulnerable ones of your children. Help us have the wisdom and courage to decide as you did in your Son, Jesus Christ. In his name we pray. Amen.

THE PRESBYTERY OF NORTH PUGET SOUND *Washington*

A new ministry has come to the Presbytery of North Puget Sound, which is composed of 34 churches with 7,688 members. Eagle Wings serves persons with disabilities by celebrating their gifts and empowering them to move toward full participation in society. In the bounds of the presbytery persons with disabilities number in the thousands. Almost half of households where a person with a disability resides have an income below $15,000, and few of those persons are employed.

Undeterred and not discouraged by the extent of the problem, the Rev. Henk Wapstra came out of retirement to establish a ministry in which he had years of experience. Eagle Wings exists to "help people fly," those people with physical disabilities and those with developmental disabilities. Churches, pastors, social service agencies, and medical personnel make referrals to the ministry. The first step is friendship building. Each person is respected as one who is made in the image of God. As a relationship with Henk builds, the needs and the gifts of each client begin to surface.

To assist churches to become intentional about utilizing the gifts of persons with disabilities, Eagle Wings provides seminars and presentations. From these gatherings often come the establishment of a church task force to evaluate what a congregation can offer. Plans include organization of an Eagle Service Club through which persons with disabilities can help others. Also planned is a disability conference of churches based on the theme "That All May Worship."

The churches of the presbytery have been enriched and motivated by Eagle Wings because it provides education and promotes awareness of the gifts of persons with disabilities. The church, among all places, needs to be at the forefront of efforts to help society benefit from the gifts and talents of all God's people. Eagle Wings points the way in the Presbytery of North Puget Sound.

Let Us Join in Prayer for:

Presbytery Staff
Dr. Terry Nelson, executive presbyter
Diana Searle, office manager
Joan Hill, administrator of finance
Dr. Paul Jensen, stated clerk
Elder Piper Eger, recording clerk

PC(USA) General Assembly Staff
Jeanette Andersen, BOP
Rev. Kathryn Anderson, WMD
Monty Anderson, PPC

Scripture
Wait for the LORD; be strong, and let your heart take courage; wait for the LORD! (Ps. 27:14).

Daily Lectionary
Ps. 27, 46 or 97, 93 or 114, 146
Isa. 52:3-6
Rev. 2:1-7; John 2:1-11

Let Us Join in Prayer for:

Presbytery Staff
Rev. Lynn Longfield, general presbyter
Susie Zych, administrative assistant
Rev. Steve Klump, treasurer
Elder Joyce Carr, stated clerk
Don McIntyre, site manager and director, Camp Sound View

PC(USA) General Assembly Staff
Robin Andres, PPC
Stacey Andres, FDN
Rev. Charles "Chip" Andrus, CMD

OLYMPIA PRESBYTERY *Washington*

The 49 churches, 2 fellowships, and 11,140 members of Olympia Presbytery are on the front lines of ministry. Beginning with its recognition that all of life and ministry belong to God, the presbytery asks prayer for those ministries where God is calling it to share resources and time.

Christians Without Borders is drawing several churches together to reach out to Hispanic immigrants in Pierce County, Washington. In partnership with Christian brothers and sisters from Mexico, Christians Without Borders also spent a week in the summer leading a Bible school and engaging the community in worship and praise of God. Sharing the gospel with each other is one way it is working to bring people together through Christ's love.

Christians Without Borders work team

A contribution from Presbyterian Disaster Assistance is giving life to a ministry with military families. Coordinated by Associated Ministries of Tacoma/Pierce County, Little Church on the Prairie in Lakewood is one among several churches in the presbytery that is offering space for this outreach to military families separated by assignment of domestic or overseas duty.

The Church of the Indian Fellowship in Tacoma is blessed with new pastoral leadership. Irving Porter, a Pima Native American and Dubuque Seminary graduate, is a commissioned lay pastor currently under the care of Olympia Presbytery. His wife, Anne-Cecile Porter, earned a master of arts in religion from Dubuque. Together they are sharing Christ's love with enthusiasm, energy, and skill.

Ps. 24:1 is indeed alive in Olympia Presbytery. Pray for the presbytery to be faithful in bringing the redemptive love of Christ to all of God's creation.

Daily Lectionary
Ps. 27, 46 or 47, 93 or 114, 147:1-11
Isa. 59:15b-21
Rev. 2:8-17; John 4:46-54

Scripture
God is our refuge and strength, a very present help in trouble (Ps. 46:1).

SEATTLE PRESBYTERY *Washington*

An interpretation of this logo can be found on the presbytery's new Web site.

Seattle Presbytery is composed of 59 congregations with 20,826 members. During a recent meeting of the presbytery, the Rev. Boyd Stockdale asked that anyone from a congregation involved in homelessness or housing mission stand up. *Everyone stood.* Although housing was not on that meeting's agenda, God was and is at work in the presbytery.

God's transforming work in Seattle Presbytery is also being expressed through communities worshiping in their own languages and customs (Hispanic, Vietnamese, Iranian, Kenyan, and Japanese). A partnership exists between Mercer Island Presbyterian Church and the Vietnamese fellowship that meets at the church to build a hospital, rehabilitation clinic, and school in Vietnam. A campus in Poulsbo is worshiping and enacting mission as an extension of Central Kitsap Presbyterian Church. Work is being done on a growing ecumenical strategy to end racism in the lives of individuals and in institutions.

Seattle Presbytery's standing rules, committee structure, mission statement, logo design, and communications are being aligned to reflect this responsive mode of mission discernment. Its new mission statement reads:

Our mission is to participate joyfully in God's transforming work through the Gospel of Jesus Christ
- *by strengthening the witness and mission of our congregations and members*
- *by building strong partnerships with each other and the larger Christian community.*

The new Spirit-Net logo was designed to facilitate connectedness, communication, and collaboration in mission. At the presbytery's innovative Web site, every user can be a contributor. Seattle Presbytery is in prayer with you and is grateful for your prayers.

Scripture

Let anyone who has an ear listen to what the Spirit is saying to the churches (Rev. 2:29).

Let Us Join in Prayer for:

Rev. Gary F. Skinner, member, GAC

Presbytery Staff
Rev. Boyd Stockdale, executive presbyter
Michelle Perry-Amos, executive assistant
Rev. Dennis J. Hughes, stated clerk
Barbara Ranta, associate stated clerk
Jeffrey Rayner, accountant/bookkeeper
Corey Schlosser-Hall, communications director
Rev. Ken Sunoo, communications assistant
Steve Sadtler, Buck Creek Camp director
Nicole Fisher, Buck Creek Camp program director
Johnnie Newell, Buck Creek Camp program assistant

Mission Volunteers in the U.S.A.
Urban Intentional Community, Young Adult Volunteers, Seattle, Washington:
Robert Fort, **Kristen Gilbert**, **Nadine Sauer**, **Shannon Smythe**, **Matthew Streeter**, and **Aaron Willett**

PC(USA) General Assembly Staff
Frank Annau, OGA
Rina Arauz, NMD
Elder Penny Arnold, FDN

Daily Lectionary

Ps. 27, 46 or 47, 93 or 114, 147:12-20
Isa. 63:1-5
Rev. 2:18-29; John 5:1-15

Let Us Join in Prayer for:

Presbytery Staff
Rev. David Dobler, executive presbyter
Elder Sharon Rayt, stated clerk
Sandy Willoughby,
administrative assistant
Mary Kron, treasurer

PC(USA) General Assembly Staff
Maria Arroyo, WMD
Peggy Ashabranner, FDN
Barbie Ashbaugh, PPC

THE PRESBYTERY OF YUKON
Alaska

The members of Gambell Presbyterian Church are preparing for their new building. With support from the community, churches of the presbytery, and partners throughout the PC(USA), this missionary congregation is on the move. The new building will provide a sanctuary and fellowship and education areas. The Gambell Presbyterian Church is an anchor of the Bering Witness mission to the Native peoples of Siberia, and its new building will enhance this vital ministry. The congregation also welcomes a new missionary, Esther Lim, infant daughter of Pastor Nathan and Rachel Lim.

The Rev. Youl Rhee and Hee Rhee serve a church in Nome, Alaska, which reaches out to several language and ethnic groups.

The Rev. Youl Rhee and his wife, Hee, are working with the Session of the Nome Presbyterian Church to redevelop this congregation. Established as a Yupik-language fellowship for natives of St. Lawrence Island who resettled on the mainland, the church now includes and reaches out to several language and ethnic groups in Nome. Presbyterian congregations in Korea are partners in this ministry.

The ministry of commissioned lay pastors (CLP) continues to grow and develop. CLP Heather Smith serves the bush congregations of the presbytery with a ministry of training and encouragement for local leaders. CLP Sandra Wagenius serves the women of Highland Mountain Correctional Facility. CLP Verna Bock continues her chaplaincy work at the Alaska Native Medical Center and participates in mission travel in Siberia with Bering Witness.

Joining with the Evangelical Lutheran Church in America and others, the presbytery is supporting an ecumenical new church development in the Big Lake area, north of Wasilla. Pastor Carin Bjorn Von Letzendorf serves the combined Presbyterian Church and Hope Lutheran Fellowship in Delta Junction.

The Presbytery of Yukon includes 3,321 members and 22 churches that worship and govern themselves in four languages (English, Inupiat, Korean, and Siberian Yupik).

Daily Lectionary

Ps. 27, 46 or 47, 93 or 114, 148
Isa. 65:1-9
Rev. 3:1-6; John 6:1-14

Scripture
Then Jesus took the loaves, and when he had given thanks, he distributed them to those who were seated; so also the fish, as much as they wanted (John 6:11).

THE SYNOD OF THE COVENANT

Three times a year people gather for twenty-four hours of rest and spiritual reflection that are part of Shared Life retreats. There are times of silence, study of Scripture, and prayer. Through the quiet, people put their lives in perspective and remember they are God's beloved. Reenergized, they go back into the world to continue their ministry.

Recently ordained pastors come together for a seven-day seminar where they reflect on their ministry and assess their calling. Hearing former attendees say "I am still in ministry because of what happened when I attended the Recently Ordained Pastors Seminar" demonstrates the need for this time away.

Partnering with the General Assembly, the synod offers incentive loans to churches that want to make life easier for their members and employees. Through accessibility loans, elevators and ramps are built so that people can enter and move around with ease in older, multiple-level buildings. Others help to keep their members warm through a loan to improve their building's energy conservation. Technology improvement loans keep communication flowing more effectively among the membership.

These synod opportunities help people live faithfully and at peace with self, each other, and God. The Synod of the Covenant includes 804 churches with 202,745 members.

Scripture

They saw Jesus walking on the sea and coming near the boat, and they were terrified. But he said to them, "It is I; do not be afraid" (John 6:19–20).

Let Us Join in Prayer for:

Synod Staff
Elder Edith Patton, interim synod executive
Rev. Larry Edwards, associate for racial ethnic and social justice ministries
Elder Diane Brasie, program staff
Elder Jack Kleier, stated clerk
Donna LeCrone, computer operations manager
Dagmar Romage, administrative assistant
Susan Allie, receptionist

PC(USA) General Assembly Staff
Luke Asikoye, WMD
Samuel Atiemo, NMD
Karen Babik, BOP

Daily Lectionary

Ps. 27, 46 or 47, 93 or 114, 149
Isa. 65:13-16
Rev. 3:7-13; John 6:15-27

THE LORD'S DAY

MINUTE FOR MISSION
BAPTISM OF THE LORD

Why did you put the baptismal font at the entrance to the sanctuary?" It is interesting how a simple move such as this one can present the opportunity for an important teachable moment. Baptism and teaching go hand in hand, and this question is a great starting point for today's lectionary readings.

The Genesis passage tells of the beginning of creation. The first element touched by God's Spirit was water. All of life began with God's Spirit moving over the water. Mark's Gospel begins with the story of Jesus being baptized by John the Baptist. Jesus' baptism marked the beginning of his ministry. Baptism, among other things, marks the beginning of a new life in Christ for all Christians.

From the time of creation, water has been a primary source of life and death. In some countries where our missionaries live and work, clean water is in short supply. The symbolism of dying and rising with Christ is extremely powerful for those whose water supplies are in danger from drought, pollution, or lack of clean water systems. Taking care of the earth's water supply should be, for all Christians, a powerful symbol of caring for God's creation. Creation began with God's Spirit and water. Our life in Christ begins with water and is lived out with God's Spirit.

Through baptism we enter the church. A baptismal font, uncovered, full of water, and at the entrance to worship, could remind us of our own baptism. Each time we gather for worship, we should be reminded of the waters that symbolize life, death, our ministry in Christ, and the connection we have through this water to all God's creation. We are also reminded that God has made us one with Christ and all who share this common bath.

—Rev. Chip Andrus, associate for worship, Theology and Worship

Prayer

Loving God, Creator of life, we give you thanks for claiming us as your own through Christ. We pray for those who struggle to live where water is in short supply. May your Spirit move in us, creating anew each day the desire to care for your earth and for those who struggle to live in this changing world. In Jesus' name. Amen.

THE PRESBYTERY OF CINCINNATI

Indiana, Kentucky, Ohio

In a changing world, the Presbytery of Cincinnati is called to proclaim and live out the good news of Jesus Christ by welcoming diversity, forming partnerships, building unity, and connecting with our communities," declares the mission statement of the Presbytery of Cincinnati, adopted in March 2001.

As an opportunity to strengthen its faith and give support to its mission statement, the Presbytery of Cincinnati was challenged with a capital campaign whose theme was "Meet You at the Table." Gifts went to urban and rural churches to improve outreach ministries, Wildwood Camp and Conference Center to foster spiritual nourishment and leadership training, peace and justice ministries to challenge relational difficulties, campus ministries to enrich young adult leadership, and new churches to grow in several areas of the presbytery.

The presbytery truly believes that the earth is the Lord's as evident in its partnership with the Presbytery of Kanh'abal in Guatemala. After an initial trip to this remote community, the presbytery hosted four Mayan pastors in August 2001. A delegation from the Presbytery of Cincinnati visited Guatemala in April 2002, continuing the exchanges in spiritual nourishment and economic development.

Young adult volunteers work with inner-city children.

The Young Adult Volunteer Program remains a vital mission project in the presbytery's urban areas. Young adults provide family crisis assistance, leadership for after-school programs, and coordination for a coffee house ministry.

Recently two historic churches, St. John's United Church of Christ and Westminster Presbyterian Church, came together in the city of Cincinnati's west side. Renamed St. John's Westminster Union Church, these two congregations are worshiping and ministering as one, while keeping their basic denominational identities.

The Presbytery of Cincinnati has 20,050 members and 84 churches.

Scripture

[God] chose us in Christ before the foundation of the world to be holy and blameless before [God] in love (Eph. 1:4).

Let Us Join in Prayer for:

Presbytery Staff
Rev. Sam Roberson, general presbyter
Rev. Yvette L. Dalton, associate general presbyter
Janis Adams, stated clerk and resource center director
Jean Snyder, administrative coordinator
Marion Montefiore, administrative assistant, office
Carol Winkler, finance coordinator
George Hufford, hunger action enabler

Mission Volunteers in the U.S.A.
Council of Urban Churches, Young Adult Volunteers, Cincinnati, Ohio: **Joann Ashley** and **Hannah Evans**

PC(USA) General Assembly Staff
Dawn Baccare, BOP
Rev. Ernesto Badillo, BOP
Joey Bailey, MSS

Daily Lectionary

Ps. 5, 29, 82, 145
Isa. 40:12-24
Eph. 1:1-14; Mark 1:1-13

Let Us Join in Prayer for:

Elder Carol Hylkema, member, GAC
Elder Helen Morrison, member, GAC

Presbytery Staff
Rev. Dr. Arlene W. Gordon, interim executive presbyter
Rev. Edward H. Koster, stated clerk
Elder Richard Grant, director outdoor ministries
Elder Joanne Higgins, resource center director
Elder Artheillia Thompson, hunger action coordinator
Elder Gerald Kruse, treasurer
Elder Beverly Knox, executive assistant
Sandra Jensen, administrative assistant
Cherisse Haugabook, financial assistant
Rhonda Roberts, clerical assistant
Sharon Johnston, office assistant

PC(USA) General Assembly Staff
Elder Marsha Bailey, NMD
Kristine Baker, EDO

THE PRESBYTERY OF DETROIT

Michigan

The Presbytery of Detroit is emerging from what began as a year of Jubilee. During this period, all committees were set aside except those required by the *Book of Order*. Operations were lodged in the presbytery council and resulted in the establishment of many work groups. Early in the year, the Process and Structure Committee was formed, and it began looking toward a new vision and mission for the presbytery. At its January meeting, the presbytery voted unanimously to accept the committee's report, which called for reshaping the way business is conducted in the presbytery, specifically giving more visibility and empowerment to congregations. It also delegated to the Staff Services Workgroup the responsibility for determining the staffing rationale for the office.

Since September 11, the presbytery has been actively involved in many ecumenical events designed to build relationships and promote understanding between various groups that make up the diverse communities in the Detroit area. The presbytery has sponsored a pre-Presbytery event to raise awareness of the beliefs and cultures of Jews and Muslims and has been involved in many ecumenical services focusing on healing and community.

The presbytery has spent a year refocusing on the spirituality of the presbytery as a whole. The office staff pauses every day at noon to pray for the entire presbytery. A spirituality network has provided monthly pre-Presbytery workshops on spiritual disciplines, and those workshops have been well attended.

Much rejoicing took place as the Hartland New Church Development (NCD) was chartered and the Filipino NCD gained momentum with the calling of a pastor. A Taiwanese fellowship has formed and is meeting regularly. Camp Howell has added three new buildings and is geared up for an exciting year of activities.

The Presbytery of Detroit is comprised of 38,230 members in 90 churches, 2 NCDs, and 2 fellowships.

Daily Lectionary

Ps. 42, 102, 133, 146
Isa. 40:25-31
Eph. 1:15-23; Mark 1:14-28

Scripture

Those who wait for the LORD shall renew their strength, they shall mount up with wings like eagles, they shall run and not be weary, they shall walk and not faint (Isa. 40:31).

EASTMINSTER PRESBYTERY

Ohio

How do we share the good news of Jesus Christ in a culture that is increasingly skeptical of institutions—especially organized religion? Many valid answers can be given to that question, but Eastminster Presbytery in northeast Ohio has answered it uniquely. A specially appointed mission task force has decided on a new church development that unfolds in an unusual way.

The mission task force envisions a mission pastor moving into the West Austintown area, a suburb of Youngstown, and meeting people where they live, work, and play. Through the outreach efforts of the mission pastor and the gathering work of the Holy Spirit, groups will begin forming in neighborhoods and meeting in homes, emerging as communities of faith as they become active in Bible study, prayer, worship, and mission.

The basic church structure will be centered on the home fellowships, so much so that a physical church building is not in the plans.

Eventually, these groups may meet in larger groups for collective worship and mission. Yet the basic church structure will be centered on the home fellowships, so much so that a physical church building is not in the plans, even if the number of people involved could build and maintain one.

Certain characteristics will be emphasized among these groups: deep, mutually edifying community; strong lay leadership; Bible study; and mission orientation. While there is no one way to be the church, the presbytery believes this way of doing/being the church has great promise for the unchurched and "church-burned."

The mission task force and the mission pastor, the Rev. Steve Fortenberry, know this model is largely untested in the PC(USA), although they know it has been effective in many parts of the non-Western world and is gaining a foothold in Western countries. They are also reminded that we trace our Christian roots back to the network of house churches founded by Paul and the other apostles.

Eastminster Presbytery includes 14,411 members and 55 congregations.

Scripture

Righteousness and justice are the foundation of your throne; steadfast love and faithfulness go before you (Ps. 89:14).

Let Us Join in Prayer for:

Rev. Danny K. Schomer, member, GAC

Presbytery Staff
Elder James W. Strang, interim executive presbyter
Rev. Mota Cramer, stated clerk
Rev. Steve Fortenberry, mission pastor
Karen and Tom Riley, directors, Joseph Badger Meadows Camp and Conference Center
Elder Pamela Sharick, administrative assistant/treasurer
Dinah Rhinehart, financial secretary
Rebecca Bodden, resource center coordinator

PC(USA) General Assembly Staff
Phoebe Baker, BOP
Zenia Baker, FDN
Johnnie Ballard, MSS

Daily Lectionary

Ps. 1, 33, 89:1-18, 147:1-11
Isa. 41:1-16
Eph. 2:1-10; Mark 1:29-45

Let Us Join in Prayer for:

Elder **Ann H. Moe**, member, GAC

Presbytery Staff
Rev. **Valerie Fargo**, associate executive
Rev. **Michael Loenshal**, stated clerk
Andrea Drapp, business
manager, treasurer
Marquietta Davis, secretary, receptionist
Sara Miller, secretary to stated clerk
Chris Wolf, resource center coordinator

PC(USA) General Assembly Staff
Stephen Ballard, BOP
Sylvia Barger, NMD
Elder **Rebecca Barnes-Davies**, NMD

THE PRESBYTERY OF LAKE HURON *Michigan*

The Presbytery of Lake Huron shares space in the new building of the Saginaw Korean Church.

I'll be selling this building, so you'll need to find another place for the presbytery office," came the clear message from the landlord. Shortly thereafter trustees and staff of the presbytery began looking at different options for new office space. No available space met the needs at a price the presbytery was willing to pay. At a trustees' meeting, inspiration struck moderator Bob Emrich. "Let's ask the Korean church if they'd be willing to add presbytery offices onto their new building." The response of the Saginaw Korean Church's pastor, Daniel Ahn, was a swift and decisive, "Yes." The result is a sensible arrangement of sharing common space. The church and the presbytery have been bountifully blessed.

Now it's time to bless native wildlife. A 50' by 50' area behind the presbytery offices will be planted in native grasses, flowers, shrubs, and trees. Why? Native plants support ten to fifty times as many species of wildlife as nonnative plants. And native plants don't need to be mowed. Minute-by-minute the average lawn mower emits ten times as many hydrocarbon pollutants as an automobile. The native plant garden will have a winding path that passes through an arbor on which American bittersweet climbs, past a patch of horsemint and golden alexanders, under the branches of a shingle oak, and past flowers blooming at different times during the summer.

God has provided the Saginaw Korean Church and the Presbytery of Lake Huron with a comfortable, inviting new home. Out of gratitude the presbytery will provide room and board for insects, bees, butterflies, birds, bats, toads, and maybe even a mouse. This is the presbytery's way of saying, "God, thank you for all your bounty, and thank you for this opportunity to restore your creation."

The Presbytery of Lake Huron has 13,235 members in 54 churches.

Daily Lectionary

Ps. 16, 62, 97, 147:12-20
Isa. 41:17-29
Eph. 2:11-22; Mark 2:1-12

Scripture
For [Christ] is our peace; in his flesh he has made both groups into one and has broken down the dividing wall, that is, the hostility between us (Eph. 2:14).

THE PRESBYTERY OF LAKE MICHIGAN *Michigan*

College students are so self-involved." Campus ministers frequently hear these words. It seems society's view of college students may be far from positive. But those who are blessed to work with them describe a group of people who haven't yet learned they can't change the world. College students see possibility where others might see a lost cause.

Supported by the 21,356 members in 70 congregations that make up the Presbytery of Lake Michigan, United Campus Ministry works with students on the campuses of Kalamazoo Valley Community College, Kalamazoo College, and Western Michigan University in Kalamazoo. These students engage in service-learning programs within and outside their community. They take trips to such places as Chicago, Philadelphia, and Mexico to learn about poverty and spend precious hours addressing the issues of poverty in their own city.

> *"I hope for a world where the dignity and well-being of all people are the highest priority, and I must work for that kind of world."*

Students speak eloquently about their desire to see people living together productively and in peace. One student who spent the weekend learning about poverty in Chicago stated, "The anger I felt in Chicago was the best kind . . . anger that inspires, empowers, clarifies your values and what you must struggle for—and against. It helps to strengthen my faith. I hope for a world where the dignity and well-being of all people are the highest priority, and I must work for that kind of world."

Another student who spent his spring break working with kids in a small Mexican village wrote, "It has been said that the kingdom of heaven is in the midst of the poor. With this thought, I remember a little girl no older than six who had nothing but a warm smile and a kind heart, whose kindness I will never forget. Long after she grows up and the memory of her youth fades, I will remember the gift she gave that day because for a moment I saw heaven in her eyes."

College students are so self-involved? No. They are involved in making this world become the place God intended for us all.

Let Us Join in Prayer for:

Rev. Linda A. Knieriemen, member, GAC

Presbytery Staff
Marilyn Benson, treasurer
Mar Mae Burch, stated clerk
Jo Fenner, office and resource center secretary
Karen Grant, administrative assistant
Karen Nottelmann, transitional associate for special ministries
Randall Painter, accounts payable manager
Jo Seppala, transitional associate for stewardship and mission
Robert Vodra, Camp Greenwood director

PC(USA) General Assembly Staff
Elder James Barnett, FDN
Alan Barthel, PAM
Andrew Bartlett, WMD
Lisa Bash, OGA

Scripture

When Jesus heard this, he said to them, "Those who are well have no need of a physician, but those who are sick; I have come to call not the righteous but sinners" (Mark 2:17).

Daily Lectionary

Ps. 51, 65, 142, 148
Isa. 42:(1-9) 10-17
Eph. 3:1-13; Mark 2:13-22

Let Us Join in Prayer for:

PC(USA) General Assembly Staff
Elder Dr. Beth Basham, EDO
Arthur Baxter, OGA
Bruce Beaver, BOP

CHRISTIAN UNITY

MINUTE FOR MISSION

"I therefore, the prisoner in the Lord, beg you to lead a life worthy of the calling to which you have been called . . . making every effort to maintain the unity of the Spirit" (Eph. 4:1–2).

Each year during the week of January 18–25, Christians from the Orthodox, Catholic, Protestant, and Pentecostal traditions celebrate the Week of Prayer for Christian Unity. As Presbyterians we diligently pray and work for the unity of the Christian church. As a demonstration of that desire, in 2006 the PC(USA) will celebrate a concurrent General Assembly with the Cumberland Presbyterian Church and the Cumberland Presbyterian Church in America in Birmingham, Alabama.

The Cumberland Presbyterian Church was organized in Tennessee in 1810. The founders of the Cumberland movement had a strong evangelical zeal. Throughout its formative years the Cumberland Presbyterian Church grew in its evangelical mission and witness as it developed schools, hospitals, and churches throughout the country. Today it has 857 churches throughout the United States and in five other countries.

In the mid-nineteenth century, social realities of the time divided the Cumberland Presbyterian Church. Founded by former slaves who sought autonomy from their owners, the Cumberland Presbyterian Church in America was organized in 1869 and constituted as a denomination in 1874. It is the first and only fully organized denomination of African Americans in the Presbyterian tradition. The Cumberland Presbyterian Church in America extends as far east as Cleveland, as far west as Dallas, and as far north as Iowa. It has over 7,000 members in 153 congregations.

Throughout our history in the United States, one of our great challenges has been to maintain the unity of the Presbyterian and Reformed churches. As we enter into this season of prayer for the unity of the church, let us be mindful of Christ's yearning for the unity of his people.

—*Rev. Carlos L. Malavé, associate, Ecumenical Relations,*
Office of the General Assembly

Daily Lectionary

Ps. 98, 104, 138, 149
Isa. (42:18-25) 43:1-13
Eph. 3:14-21; Mark 2:23–3:6

Prayer

Three in One! Unite the hearts of your people, and reveal to them your great purpose. Leave them not to themselves, but guide their steps by the light of your Spirit, and cheer their hearts by your love. Only you are their Helper and their Lord. In Jesus' name. Amen.

THE LORD'S DAY

MINUTE FOR MISSION
EVANGELICAL SEMINARY OF PUERTO RICO

Ah! seminary life . . . This is the period in your life when you encounter vast amounts of knowledge and experiences. And you want to share all of it with everyone. There is a problem, though. You approach congregations and parishioners with all of the exegetical phrases, hermeneutical approaches, homiletical discourses, this-is-the-correct-way-to-do-it apologetics, and so on, and the response you hear is: "Can something good (and intelligible) come from seminary?"

Unquestionably, seminaries change lives. Just as Nathaniel questioned Philip on Nazareth's reputation, people often will ask questions among themselves about our seminaries' mission, vision, students, professors, and teaching. Certainly, many of us have been persuaded by God's voice even before entering the Evangelical Seminary of Puerto Rico's gates. Others, like Philip, have heard the voice explicitly say "follow me" even before knowing there is such an institution as the seminary.

> *Seminaries change lives, and we pray that those changed lives can keep this beautiful cycle going—to keep changing lives.*

Ah! seminary life . . . This is the time when many of us feel like Samuel, sometimes doubting the call that he eventually will respond to as, "Speak, for your servant is listening" (1 Sam. 3:10). This is the time when we empathize with the psalmist, when even though we can intellectualize, our thoughts are eager to hear God's voice, understanding that God is familiar with our ways, "even before a word" is on our tongues (Ps. 139:4). Seminaries change lives, and we pray that those changed lives can keep this beautiful cycle going—to keep changing lives.

—*Julio R. Vargas-Vidal, graduating seminarian, administrative assistant to the Development Office*

Prayer

Christ, we pray for the mission accomplished by the diverse theological education institutions you have established. Since everything in the earth is yours, we are committed to serve all who live on it. We pray and affirm different points of view and diverse approaches in mission. We thank you for diversity and for enabling us to heed that invitation you once gave us. We ask for strength in facing criticisms and lack of understanding aimed at us. May the world know that surely good things can come out of our own Nazareths. In your name. Amen.

Sunday Lectionary and Hymns

1 Sam. 3:1–10 (11–20)
Lord, When I Came Into This Life
PH 522

Ps. 139:1–6, 13–18
You Are Before Me, Lord
PH 248; PPCS 143

1 Cor. 6:12–20
Lord Jesus, Think on Me
PH 301; HB 270

John 1:43–51
Lord, You Have Come to the Lakeshore
PH 377

Daily Lectionary

Ps. 19, 81, 113, 150
Isa. 43:14–44:5
Heb. 6:17–7:10; John 4:27-42

THE PRESBYTERY OF MACKINAC
Michigan

Let Us Join in Prayer for:

Presbytery Staff
Rev. David Van Dam, presbytery executive
Lindy Bearss, administrative assistant
Elder Harry Begley, stated clerk
Beach Hall, treasurer

PC(USA) General Assembly Staff
Edwin Beck, OGA
Rev. Elizabeth Beckhusen, DEDO
Joy Begley, DEDO

The natural beauty of northern Michigan, with its outdoor recreational opportunities, prompted the Presbytery of Mackinac to consider establishing leisure ministry churches that would reach out to people on vacation who wanted to worship in a Presbyterian church. Two such churches were started in this way.

Church in the Hills, Bellaire, was built as a house, and it was understood that if the church's mission did not work, the house could be sold. For years the church struggled, and at one point the house was put up for sale. But the presbytery decided to wait one more year before closing it, and the congregation, with new leadership and God's help, began to grow as it reached out to permanent residents. In a few years, the mortgage on the original building was paid

photo by the Rev. David Van Dam

Church in the Hills, Bellaire, is now a flourishing church.

off, the sanctuary was remodeled and enlarged, and an educational unit was added. The membership has flourished. This community church still reaches out to area resorts, summer lake residents, young families, and retired people.

Over the rolling, wooded hills of northern Michigan, another leisure ministry church was established. Michaywe Presbyterian was named for the local resort community, and it became associated with those who used the golf course. An interim pastor suggested the church's name be changed. Today, First Presbyterian of Gaylord has a full-time pastor and a congregation that has grown so that an addition is being planned. The congregation is composed mainly of retired people and seasonal residents, but the church is reaching out to younger families.

Although both churches began primarily to serve people on vacation, two vital congregations have grown from them and are now part of the community of permanent residents.

The Presbytery of Mackinac serves 7,426 members in 42 churches.

Scripture
There is one body and one Spirit . . . one Lord, one faith, one baptism, one God and Father of all, who is above all and through all and in all (Eph. 4:4–6).

Daily Lectionary

Ps. 97, 112, 135, 145
Isa. 44:6-8, 21-23
Eph. 4:1-16; Mark 3:7-19a

MAUMEE VALLEY PRESBYTERY

Ohio, Michigan

Though Ps. 24:1 proclaims that "the earth is the LORD's and all . . . those who live in it," we know that not all of God's people share equally in the abundance of living. To provide for the needs of some of those, Maumee Valley Presbytery, in conjunction with the Synod of the Covenant and the Ohio Migrant Education Center, provides two weeks of health fairs

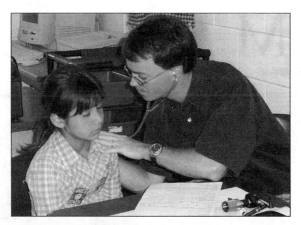

A doctor checks the heart and lungs of a young girl at a health fair.

for migrant workers who come to northwest Ohio and southern Michigan to work in the fields of cucumbers, tomatoes, and other crops. In 2001 nine health fairs served 644 persons. Most of those helped were children enrolled in migrant schools. Volunteers from churches assisted the synod team in testing vision, hearing, and blood pressure and in other necessary duties. Physicians, dentists, hygienists, and nurses tested for medical and dental problems.

Dr. Earl McLoney and Dr. Richard Blake were among the physicians at one of the health fairs. In addition to the on-site volunteers, many church groups throughout the presbytery provided health care and dental kits for the migrant workers. Donations from Maumee Valley Presbytery enabled the Ohio Migrant Education Center to provide follow-up medical and dental care.

Maumee Valley Presbytery has a working relationship with Berea Presbytery in Mexico. Two representatives of Berea Presbytery, the Rev. Hazael Campuzano and the Rev. Armando Pacheco, both from Mexico City, offered valuable services at the health fairs in Maumee Valley Presbytery. They provided translation assistance, taught children, shared their faith with the migrant workers, and helped put a friendly face on the health fairs and on this mission of the church.

Maumee Valley Presbytery serves 14,612 members in 81 churches.

Scripture

And looking at those who sat around him, he said, "Here are my mother and my brothers! Whoever does the will of God is my brother and sister and mother" (Mark 3:34–35).

Let Us Join in Prayer for:

Presbytery Staff
Elder Hilary N. Shuford, general presbyter
Rev. Dean McGormley, stated clerk
Beth Wenner, secretary for administration
Jane Hedges, secretary for presbytery mission

PC(USA) General Assembly Staff
Joseph Bell, BOP
Morton Bell, OGA
Serrita Bell, FDN

Daily Lectionary

Ps. 30, 86, 123, 146
Isa. 44:9-20
Eph. 4:17-32; Mark 3:19b-35

Let Us Join in Prayer for:

Presbytery Staff
Elder Margaret Haney,
executive presbyter
Rev. Katherine Horne, interim associate
Rev. Ed DeLair, associate executive
Rev. Doris Whitaker, stated clerk
Rev. Jayne Ruiz, Hispanic ministries
Elder Pat Turner, office manager
Elder Martha Kienzle, resource center
Elder Terry Biers, resource center
Pat McLaughlin, resource center
Elder Joyce Routzohn, support staff

PC(USA) General Assembly Staff
DeeDee Belmar, PPC
Beth Bensman, OGA
Kirsten Benson, WMD

Daily Lectionary

Ps. 4, 15, 48, 147:1-11
Isa. 44:24–45:7
Eph. 5:1-14; Mark 4:1-20

MIAMI PRESBYTERY

Ohio

Miami Presbytery is seeking new ways to be God's people sent into the world. In partnership with its Hispanic neighbors, the presbytery is building a holistic ministry that provides practical and spiritual resources. Congregations are responding to God's call for the church to reach out to the rapidly growing Hispanic community in their midst in new and creative ways.

Christmas in October is one of the annual projects of Presbyterian Women. Personal care items and other gifts are brought to the Fall Gathering and donated to Mount Pleasant and Dorothy Love, the two Presbyterian retirement communities in the area.

Heritage Presbyterian Church's volunteer tutors and their students show that learning can be fun!

Churches large and small are serving their communities. Heritage Presbyterian Church, with ninety-one members, has begun an after-school tutoring program. Weekly communication between teachers and volunteers is key to this partnership. Teachers are unanimous about the positive influence this program has had on the children's lives. Genuine love has grown between the children and the volunteers.

Westminster Presbyterian Church, with 1,271 members, and Van Cleve Elementary School have a seven-year partnership. The church supports the school in several ways that benefit students, their families, and the school faculty, including grants for classroom improvements. The church hosts tutoring twice a week, Student of the Month Lunches, and a year-end Celebrate Learning Dinner for teachers, students, their families, tutors, and school board members. The success of this partnership inspired an effort to entice other schools and churches to form their own partnerships, and ten pairings have been launched so far.

There are 16,674 members in the 65 churches of Miami Presbytery.

Scripture

I will both lie down and sleep in peace; for you alone, O LORD, make me lie down in safety (Ps. 4:8).

THE PRESBYTERY OF MUSKINGUM VALLEY *Ohio*

To acknowledge that the earth belongs to God is to recognize that those who live in it are stewards. The 97 congregations of the Presbytery of Muskingum Valley with their 14,589 members serve as stewards in a variety of ways from their east central Ohio location.

The Fellowship of Christ's Community practices stewardship through its vegetable garden project. The fellowship, directed by Sister Nadine Overbeck, O.S.F., is a gathering of low-income families that meets on Sunday evenings for alternative worship at Central Presbyterian Church in Zanesville. After a farmer nearby plows a corner of his field, members work the ground, plant the seeds, weed and water the garden, and gather the harvest. The vegetables are served at the Sunday evening meal before worship. Some are canned or frozen for the winter months, some are carried home, and the rest are shared with other area food ministries.

As the garden crew rediscovers God's good earth, children at Camp Presmont, at the opposite end of the presbytery, learn to enjoy and take care of God's world during camp sessions. One session pairs children and their parents at a fishing camp.

Other Presbyterians are acting as stewards of God's earth within the presbytery. Students

Members of the Fellowship of Christ's Community till their vegetable garden.

from the College of Wooster and Muskingum College work toward improving people and land relationships through their various mission projects. Several churches are stewards of natural resources by becoming ENERGY STAR congregations. Unity Presbyterian Church in Cambridge discovered it could lower its energy usage by installing a temperature setback sensor to control the furnace's heat output and by repairing latches so windows close completely. Environmental concerns are lifted up during worship on the Sunday closest to Earth Day. Elder Quentin Knauer is the presbytery's Restoring Creation Enabler.

Scripture
How precious is your steadfast love, O God! All people may take refuge in the shadow of your wings (Ps. 36:7).

Let Us Join in Prayer for:

Presbytery Staff
Elder David E. Meerse, interim executive presbyter
Rev. Virginia Birks, stated clerk and interim associate
Janet L. Thomas, administrative assistant
Linda Nacci, resource center assistant
Teresa Prouty, coordinator, financial services

PC(USA) General Assembly Staff
Deborah Bernard, BOP
Jacqueline Besco, BOP
Leslie Bethell, CMD

Daily Lectionary
Ps. 27, 36, 80, 147:12-20
Isa. 45:5-17
Eph. 5:15-33; Mark 4:21-34

Week of Prayer for Christian Unity

THE PRESBYTERY OF SCIOTO VALLEY *Ohio*

Let Us Join in Prayer for:

Presbytery Staff
Rev. Dana Knapp, executive presbyter
Elder Jeannie Harsh, Christian
educator/resource center coordinator
Elder James A. Wilson, stated clerk
Pat Rose, presbytery office coordinator
Ed Hoeflinger, financial secretary
Pamela Ramage, camp administrator
Danya Platt, camp outdoor
education coordinator
Carl Gehret, camp site manager/naturalist
Angie Hill, camp office manager

PC(USA) General Assembly Staff
Barbara Betts, MSS
Shena Bibb, MSS

I n the Presbytery of Scioto Valley, there is no better way to be renewed in the Spirit than by spending time at the Geneva Hills Center, where one can truly associate the psalmist's words, "I lift up my eyes to the hills—from where will my help come? My help comes from the LORD, who made heaven and earth" (Ps. 121:1–2).

God's abundant love and grace are present while participants commune with nature at Geneva Hills Center, the camp and retreat ministry of, for, and by the congregations that make up the presbytery. Open to all who seek the benefit of this mission-based environment, the center has year-round programming and offers opportunities for spiritual growth, education, recreation, and fellowship for individuals and groups.

The Geneva Hills Center is a place where God's natural environment joins with human leadership to provide a significant place of support and growth.

Canoeing and kayaking are available at Geneva Hills Center.

Located on over three hundred acres of rolling hills that include forest, fields, a lake, a pond, hiking trails, and an outdoor pool, Geneva Hills is in a natural habitat where wildlife communicates to youth and adults alike and where common and holy ground are available to all God's Creation.

The facilities of the camp and retreat center encourage spiritual renewal through numerous educational and recreational opportunities. The camps provide a place for church staff to do team building and leadership development. Individuals and groups are challenged by working their way through initiative and ropes courses and a climbing wall. Geneva Hills offers summer and winter camps, weekend retreats, and family camps and programs.

The 26,351 members and 112 churches of the Presbytery of Scioto Valley are blessed by having Geneva Hills Center in their midst.

Daily Lectionary

Ps. 32, 130, 139, 148
Isa. 45:18-25
Eph. 6:1-9; Mark 4:35-41

Scripture
Turn to me and be saved, all the ends of the earth! For I am God, and there is no other (Isa. 45:22).

THE PRESBYTERY OF THE WESTERN RESERVE *Ohio*

Located in northeast Ohio, the Presbytery of the Western Reserve includes 54 congregations that engage 15,811 Presbyterians in ministry and mission. The presbytery encompasses urban, suburban, and rural communities, offering a wide range of opportunities for members with diverse backgrounds, skills, and interests to be faithful disciples of Jesus Christ.

photo by Ida Pinkava

Musicians lead members of the presbytery in song at The Highlands Camp and Conference Center.

A rich resource for education and community, The Highlands Camp and Conference Center is in the eastern region of the presbytery near Middlefield, in the heart of Amish country. In August 2003, people of all ages will gather at The Highlands to consider God's call to all people as stewards of the earth. Participants will study biblical themes of creation and stewardship in light of many environmental issues that confront society.

"Seeing the Earth from Another Perspective" will be the theme of this residential camping experience. Each day will include worship and Bible study and opportunities to explore God's hand in the creation of lakes, forests, and meadows; to observe both constellations and satellites in the night sky; and to celebrate the earth through music, art, and poetry. Conservation and natural resources experts from the region will augment the conference leadership team to provide unique experiences, including the remote sensing of the earth guided by NASA specialists.

Restoring Creation Enablers for the presbytery, the Rev. Lynn Anderson and Elder Harold Barton, interpret programs and partnerships that encourage faithful stewardship. Partnerships with other groups and individuals make it possible for congregations to explore in a variety of ways what it means to live in light of the psalmist's declaration, "The earth is the LORD's."

Scripture

Be strong in the Lord and in the strength of his power. Put on the whole armor of God, so that you may be able to stand against the wiles of the devil (Eph. 6:10–11).

Let Us Join in Prayer for:

Presbytery Staff
Rev. Elizabeth G. Hendricks, general presbyter
Rev. Lynn Anderson, director, The Highlands Camp and Conference Center
Elder Laura Steidel, staff associate
Elder Twana Reeves, staff associate
Rev. Douglas J. Tracy, stated clerk
Rev. Susan W. Holderness, pastor to clergy and families
Elder Lee Lohr, staff associate and campaign administrator
Ken LaRosse, site manager of The Highlands

PC(USA) General Assembly Staff
Elder Beneva Bibbs, NMD
Robert Binelli, BOP

Daily Lectionary

Ps. 56, 111, 118, 149
Isa. 46:1-13
Eph. 6:10-24; Mark 5:1-20

Sunday Lectionary and Hymns

Jon. 3:1–5, 10
My Lord! What a Morning
PH 449

Ps. 62:5–12
I to the Hills Will Lift My Eyes
PH 234; HB 377; PPCS 52

1 Cor. 7:29–31
God of Grace and God of Glory
PH 420; HB 358

Mark 1:14–20
How Clear Is Our Vocation, Lord
PH 419

Daily Lectionary

Ps. 46, 67, 93, 150
Isa. 47:1-15
Heb. 10:19-31; John 5:2-18

THE LORD'S DAY

MINUTE FOR MISSION
PRINCETON THEOLOGICAL SEMINARY

Professor J. Wentzel van Huyssteen, the James I. McCord Professor of Theology and Science at Princeton Theological Seminary, teaches his students that Christian theology fundamentally believes that "nothing in this world, and in our universe, is completely understood until we also understand it as God's good creation: In this sense the spectacular recent scientific discoveries about the age and origins of the universe open new doors for theology to redescribe and reinterpret these exciting new theories in light of Scripture."

Since its founding in 1812, Princeton Seminary has taught the interpretation of the Bible as sacred Scripture for God's people. Today, as the twenty-first century dawns, Princeton's faculty and students also study the scientific wonders of the universe—from tiny molecules of DNA in the human body to vast galaxies in outer space—as they, too, reveal a loving Creator God.

Faculty like Dr. van Huyssteen; Dr. Max Stackhouse, who heads the new Abraham Kuyper Center, which was created to address the intersection of theology, ecology, and technology; and Dr. Nancy Duff, who explores the ethics of human reproduction, cloning, sexuality, and other spiritual issues in medicine, teach students to understand and care for the vast universe God has created.

Through such events as a national videoconference featuring van Huyssteen and British scientist Sir John Polkinghorne, Princeton's Center of Continuing Education explores how theologians and scientists understand what it means to be human, or made in the image of God. The Kuyper Center hosts conferences like one in 2002 on the relationship of concepts of nature, the environment, and the transformation offered by technology.

Such events, courses, and conversations continue the ancient dialogue begun by the psalmist long ago: "When I look at your heavens, the work of your fingers, the moon and the stars that you have established; what are human beings that you are mindful of them . . . ? Yet you have made them a little lower than God, and crowned them with glory and honor" (Ps. 8:3–5).

—Dr. Thomas W. Gillespie, president, Princeton Theological Seminary

Prayer
Lord, our sovereign, how majestic is your name in all the earth. May we wonder at the earth and the universe, always in praise of you, the Creator. And may we be good stewards of the earth and of our own minds and of the knowledge that you have given us to discover the universe's treasures and mysteries. We pray this in the name of Jesus Christ, who was before the beginning, is now, and ever will be. Amen.

CENTRAL AND WEST AFRICA

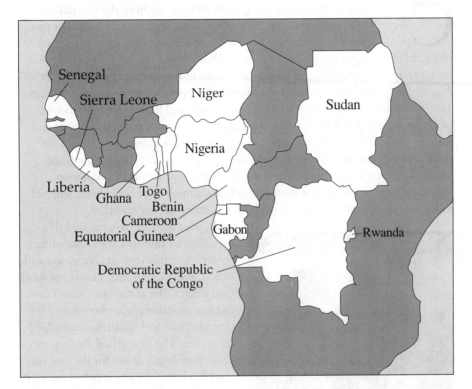

Let Us Join in Prayer for:

Partners/Ministries
All Africa Conference of Churches:
The Very Rev. Dr. Kwesi Dickson,
president, **Mr. Melaku Kifle**, interim
general secretary; Project for
Christian-Muslim Relations in
Africa (PROCMURA): **Rev. Dr. Johnson
Mbillah**, general adviser

PC(USA) General Assembly Staff
Julia Binger, NMD
Bobbi Binggeli, DEDO
Gail Bingham, WMD

The earth is the LORD's and all . . . those who live in it." This verse speaks to me of an abundance of life through sharing in God's creation, both in physical and spiritual terms. I invite you to consider deeply the implications that are bound in this verse for the people of Central and West Africa. How do the people in that region of the world experience life and share in God's creation? What is our relationship and responsibility to our brothers and sisters there? We highlight in these pages the nine countries in which the Presbyterian Church (U.S.A.) has ongoing church-to-church relations—or partnerships. You may have friends or interests in one of the other countries in this region as well and will reflect on them.

Scripture
[Jesus] said to her, "Daughter, your faith has made you well; go in peace, and be healed of your disease" (Mark 5:34).

Daily Lectionary
Ps. 47, 57, 85, 145
Isa. 48:1-11
Gal. 1:1-17; Mark 5:21-43

Let Us Join in Prayer for:

PC(USA) General Assembly Staff
Anne Blair, WMD
Whitney Blair, MSS
Elder Ben Blake, PILP

CENTRAL AND WEST AFRICA
continued

Consider that 13 percent of the world's refugees are from the Central and West Africa region and that 25 percent of the countries in the world that produce refugees are in this region. There are over nine million internally displaced and refugee people in the region. Almost three million people have died in the Democratic Republic of Congo as a result of the war that began there in August 1998. You will remember that 800,000 people died in Rwanda in the early 1990s, but do you realize that a true reconciliation and healing have yet to take place among the people? In Sudan, the people of the south still seek equality and justice—and still run for cover when their government's planes drop bombs on their schools, hospitals, and churches. Many people are losing their homes and land as international interests systematically deplete the forests of Cameroon. Young children across coastal West Africa find themselves on boats being shipped to live out their lives in some foreign land as someone's "houseworker."

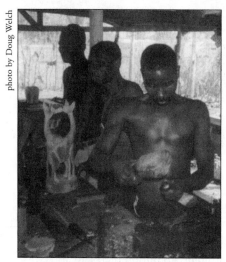

photo by Doug Welch

Students develop carpentry skills as part of the Evangelical Presbyterian Church of Ghana's woodworking project.

On your behalf I have traveled this region, and I find that tears flow when I contemplate this verse in connection with what I have experienced. This is not what God desires. But at the same time I can think of no other place where true expressions of faith and reliance on God are greater. The Evangelical Presbyterian Church of Togo's theme for the past two years has been "the whole gospel for every person," and the church is working hard to share this message across the country. Education for everyone is the focus of the Evangelical Church of Niger as its members are energized to share throughout the country the good news of Jesus Christ. In Cameroon, people are joining together to speak out against the destruction of forests and the lives and homes of many villagers.

Daily Lectionary

Ps. 28, 54, 99, 146
Isa. 48:12-21 (22)
Gal. 1:18–2:10; Mark 6:1-13

Scripture
The LORD is the strength of [the] people; [the Lord] is the saving refuge of [the] anointed (Ps. 28:8).

CENTRAL AND WEST AFRICA
continued

Volunteer evangelists in Sudan walk fifteen to twenty miles from village to village carrying the "Jesus" film, a projector, and a generator in order to make the good news known to every person in that country. Even with hunger and disorder in Congo's capital, Kinshasa, the church there is actively engaged in telling the forest people, or pygmies, of God's love for them. The street children of Kigali, Rwanda, made homeless when their parents were killed in the genocide, have a home and an opportunity to learn and grow due to the efforts of the Presbyterian Church in Rwanda. The Presbyterian Church of Nigeria has twenty-two mission workers across the country and in neighboring countries in an effort to spread the gospel. Story after story can be told about people of deep faith and of their efforts to make Christ known to every person. The PC(USA) supports each of these ministries financially and through the presence of mission personnel.

A Presbyterian Church of Nigeria choir praises God's marvelous works.

photo by Doug Welch

As you reflect and pray through the following days, think about how the people of Central and West Africa experience life and experience the Lord. Rejoice with them in the amazing ways in which God is using them for Christian ministry, even in the face of adversity. Pray for them and the churches as they seek to share God's love through Jesus Christ. Pray for ourselves so that our witness for Christ might be as vibrant and real as those of our brothers and sisters in Central and West Africa!

—*Douglas M. Welch, area coordinator for Central and West Africa*

Scripture
It is no longer I who live, but it is Christ who lives in me. And the life I now live in the flesh I live by faith in the Son of God, who loved me and gave himself for me (Gal. 2:20).

Let Us Join in Prayer for:

PC(USA) General Assembly Staff
Elder Phillip Blake, FDN
Betsy Blocker, PILP
Dennis Blum, MSS

Daily Lectionary
Ps. 65, 91, 125, 147:1-11
Isa. 49:1-12
Gal. 2:11-21; Mark 6:13-29

Let Us Join in Prayer for:

PC(USA) People in Mission
Presbyterian Church in Cameroon (EPC):
Anna L. Bauerband, theological educator,
Larry C. Bauerband, theological educator,
Inge Lise Sthreshley, consultant in
community health projects, **Lawrence
Leonard Sthreshley**, consultant in
community health projects, Presbyterian
Church in Cameroon; **Jeffrey Scott Boyd**,
Central Africa Mission Enabler,
Presbyterian Church (U.S.A.);
Petra Christi Boyd, companionship
facilitator, Joining Hands Against Hunger
Network; **Caryl I. Weinberg**, Central and
West Africa HIV/AIDS consultant

Partners/Ministries
EPC: **Rev. Nyansako-Ni-Nku**, moderator,
Rev. Dr. Festus Asana, general secretary;
Dager Theological Seminary; Church
Development and Evangelism Program;
Kumba Theological Seminary; Protestant
Church of Africa; Presbytery Partnerships:
Presbytery of Chicago with the Network to
Fight Against Hunger in Cameroon;
Presbytery of St. Andrew with the EPC

PC(USA) General Assembly Staff
Michele Blum, PPC
Claudia Bodine, CMD

Daily Lectionary

Ps. 81, 116, 143, 147:12-20
Isa. 49:13-23 (24-26); Gal. 3:1-14
Mark 6:30-46

CAMEROON

In January 2002, Fadimatou Djara found a marker in her orchard. An intruder had driven a short post into the ground. Its message said she would be expropriated of her garden, the revenue from which has provided for her family. Her five mango, seven avocado, and seven banana trees have to make way for the Chad-Cameroon oil pipeline, a project of a consortium made up of Exxon, Chevron, and Petronas, Malaysia's state oil company. Most likely her house will be taken. Her consent was not solicited, nor has compensation been addressed.

Fadimatou's story came from mission co-worker Christi Boyd, who works with the Network for the Fight Against Hunger (RELUFA), sponsored by the Presbyterian Hunger Program. This network advocates economic justice and has brought together an ecumenical group of churches, nonprofit organizations, and grassroots groups in Cameroon that are committed to all aspects of the fight against hunger.

photo by Christi Boyd

An indigenous Bakola (pygmy) family are among the people marginalized by the effects of globalization.

The Djara family is but one of many on the 1,070-kilometer (663-mile) track set out for the pipeline to transport oil from its source in neighboring Chad to Cameroon's small coastal fishing town of Kribi. From there it will be exported. Along the way the pipeline will have a major impact on the settlements of marginalized Baka, Bakola, and Bagyeli pygmy people groups who live in Cameroon's tropical forests. "The pipeline will deprive them of the necessities for the preservation of their particular and already endangered way of life. Not only the oil, but most of the revenue will leave the country, leaving many Cameroonians like Fadimatou empty-handed," writes Ms. Boyd. Through organizations like RELUFA, Presbyterians are helping to fight unjust economic and political forces that abandon the interests of the poor.

Total Area: 181,000 sq. mi. (slightly larger than California). **Population**: 15,803,220. **Languages**: 24 major African language groups, English and French (official). **GDP Per Capita**: $1,700. **Literacy**: 63.4% (Male 75%, Female 52.1%). **Religions**: indigenous beliefs, Christian, Muslim. **Life Expectancy**: 54.59 years. **Human Development Index Rank**: 125.

Scripture
Sing for joy, O heavens, and exult, O earth; break forth, O mountains, into singing! For the LORD has comforted [the] people, and will have compassion on [the] suffering ones (Isa. 49:13).

DEMOCRATIC REPUBLIC OF THE CONGO

photo by Mike Haninger

School children with Nancy Haninger eagerly await the completion of their new school.

Adversaries in the Democratic Republic of the Congo's (DRC) nearly four-year war met for the first time in March 2002 to begin talks aimed at bringing peace and political unity to the nation. The talks ended in April without the parties reaching agreement. It is feared that the collapse of the talks could reignite war in the DRC.

The churches of the DRC struggle with how to minister, with limited resources, to the immense physical and spiritual needs of people who have been impoverished and oppressed for more than four decades. Dr. Michael and Nancy Haninger, mission co-workers at the Good Shepherd Hospital, partner with the Presbyterian Community of Congo in that struggle.

The Haningers share the day-to-day existence of the villagers in Tshikaji. "'Meme, ndi ne,' is Tshiluba for 'I have' or literally, 'me, I am with.' The language tells a story. I am with something today. It is not mine but only for me to use today. The people do not hoard but have for today what they need for today. The Bible says, 'Do not lay up for yourselves treasures upon earth where moth and rust destroy and where thieves break in and steal.' This is a way of life for people in Tshikaji. What the forces of nature and the insects don't destroy, the unpaid soldiers will steal for their own survival. It is not possible to romanticize the reality of life when you have seen their existence. We feel blessed to walk with our brothers and sisters down their paths, visit their homes, and share a meal with them. We offer you the wish of the people of the village: that your lives are joyful."

Total Area: 874,500 sq. mi. (slightly less than one-fourth the size of the United States). **Population**: 53,624,718. **Languages**: French (official), Lingala, Kingwana, Kikongo, Tshiluba. **GDP Per Capita**: $600. **Literacy**: 77.3% (Male 86.6%, Female 67.7%). **Religions**: Roman Catholic, Protestant, Kimbanguist, Muslim, other syncretic sects and indigenous beliefs. **Life Expectancy**: 48.94 years. **Human Development Index Rank**: 142.

Scripture

The Lord GOD has given me the tongue of a teacher, that I may know how to sustain the weary with a word. Morning by morning [the Lord] wakens—wakens my ear to listen as those who are taught (Isa. 50:4).

Let Us Join in Prayer for:

PC(USA) People in Mission
Christian Medical Institute of the Kasai, Kananga (IMCK): **Dr. Michael Kevin Haninger**, OB/GYN-physician, **Nancy Carol Haninger**, team ministry; Presbyterian Community of Congo (DRC): **Sue Sager**, team ministry, **Dr. William Joseph Sager**, medical doctor at IMCK, **Bonnie Louise Stephens**, team ministry, **Rev. Gerald Austin Stephens, Jr.**, Christian education consultant

PC(USA) General Assembly Staff
Elder Ruth Anne Boklage, DEDO
Tonda Bonmon, MSS
Jo Ann Booker, FDN
Margaret Hall Boone, CMD

Daily Lectionary

Ps. 6, 20, 88, 148
Isa. 50:1-11
Gal. 3:15-22; Mark 6:47-56

Let Us Join in Prayer for:

PC(USA) People in Mission
Rev. Diana Christine Wright,
evangelist/church administrator,
Reformed Presbyterian Church of
Equatorial Guinea (RPCEG)

Partners/Ministries
Church of Christ in Congo (ECC)
[Congo]: **Dr. Marini**, president; Université
Protestante au Congo: **Rev. Dr. Ngoy
Boliya**, dean; Presbyterian Community
of Kinshasa (CPK) [Congo]:
Rev. Tshimungu Mayele, general
secretary; Presbyterian Community of
Congo (CPC): **Rev. Dr. Mulumba M.
Mukundi**, general secretary, **Rev. Bope
Mikobi**, legal representative,
Rev. Tshibemba Tshimpaka, legal
representative; Christian Presbyterian
Hospital, Mbujimayi [Congo]; Christian
Medical Institute of the Kasai (IMCK)
[Congo]: **Bernard Kabibu**, administrator;
Bibanga, Bulape, Lubondai, Luebo, and
Mutoto hospitals [Congo]; Presbytery
Partnerships: Presbytery of Eastern Virginia
with the CPK; Presbytery of Whitewater
Valley with the CPC; RPCEG: **Rev. Juan
Ebang Ela**, general secretary

PC(USA) General Assembly Staff
Elder Anthony Booth, DEDO
Rev. Dr. Steven A. Boots, NMD

Daily Lectionary

Ps. 63, 100, 122, 149
Isa. 51:1-8
Gal. 3:23-29; Mark 7:1-23

DEMOCRATIC REPUBLIC OF THE CONGO, *continued*

Struggle with Hope

Mission co-workers Dr. Bill and Sue Sager of Good Shepherd Hospital talk about the struggle between their expectations and the reality of life in the Democratic Republic of the Congo. "We are experiencing and wrestling with issues of poverty that transcend any awareness and experience we have ever known. We have nearly given up hope of being able to influence or change the things that we came here prepared and determined to do. The harder we try to evaluate, diagnose, and treat the problems (the major hurdles are not necessarily medical), the more difficult the path.

"In fact, after many months of struggle we find ourselves at the very beginning, but, as Maria von Trapp says in *The Sound of Music*, 'It's a very good place to start.' With this in mind, and with the assurances of God's promises, we will keep trying."

EQUATORIAL GUINEA

In the United States the 1850s were a time of exploration and pioneering. As people moved west to discover land and gold, Presbyterian missionaries went to Africa. They established one of the first Presbyterian churches in the country we now know as Equatorial Guinea. The Reformed Presbyterian Church of Equatorial Guinea (RPCEG) has been an important Protestant presence since then, but when the country gained its independence from Spain in the 1960s, the missionaries returned to the United States.

The Rev. Diana Wright, one of the first mission co-workers to be sent at the request of the RPCEG in over thirty years, is helping to rebuild bridges. She works with the Rev. Juan Ebang Ela, the general secretary of the RPCEG, in administration and work with spiritual development and renewal for pastors. Presbyterians in both the United States and Equatorial Guinea are rejoicing that this historically important relationship has been reestablished.

Total Area: 10,800 sq. mi. (slightly smaller than Maryland). **Population**: 486,060. **Languages**: Spanish and French (official), pidgin English, Fang, Bubi, Ibo. **GDP Per Capita**: $2,000. **Literacy**: 78.5% (Male 89.6%, Female 68.1%). **Religions**: nominally Christian and predominantly Roman Catholic, pagan practices. **Life Expectancy**: 53.95 years. **Human Development Index Rank**: 110.

Scripture

As many of you as were baptized into Christ have clothed yourselves with Christ. There is no longer Jew or Greek, there is no longer slave or free, there is no longer male and female; for all of you are one in Christ Jesus (Gal. 3:27–28).

THE LORD'S DAY

MINUTE FOR MISSION
RACE RELATIONS

The 213th General Assembly (2001) adopted at its gathering in Louisville, Kentucky, Commissioner's Resolution 01-3, which called on the Presbyterian Church (U.S.A.) to
- confess the corporate guilt the Presbyterian Church (U.S.A.) shares for the evils of slavery and request forgiveness from God and from all God's children whose lives have been damaged by these sins, and
- pledge and promise to seek, through words and deeds, as individuals and as a denomination, to demonstrate our sorrow by committing ourselves to work with our African American brothers and sisters to overcome the vestiges of slavery that manifest themselves today in the church and society as racism.

What does it mean to apologize for the historic legacy of slavery? Does it mean to continue with business as usual or to move in a new direction? Amos 5:21–25 makes it unmistakably clear that God wants justice, not empty-hearted apologies, promises, and worship. The Assembly pledged to demonstrate in words and actions a renewed commitment to overcome vestiges of racism in church and society. This pledge indicates a desire to move in a radically new direction. Much of the outcome of this apology depends on what happens in congregations.

Congregations can start on this journey of understanding by establishing education classes and dialogue on the relationship between slavery and contemporary racism. If the church of Jesus Christ is to overcome racism, it must first understand the historic context that gave rise to it and still nurtures it. For information on how this may be done, visit the PC(USA) Web page, Racial Ethnic Ministries, Racial Justice, or contact the Office for Racial Justice Policy Development.

—*Rev. Otis Turner, associate, Racial Justice/Policy Development*

Prayer
Call to Renewal

We gather as a community of faith seeking to live the unity that is ours in Christ.
We gather as sisters and brothers striving to share life with all of its joys and sorrows.
We gather celebrating the diversity of the human family God creates.
We gather to love one another as God loves us.
We gather to worship God.
We gather to make real the promises we have made to those who continue to suffer from our actions and inactions. In Jesus' name. Amen.

Sunday Lectionary and Hymns

Deut. 18:15–20
Thanks to God Whose Word Was Written
PH 331

Ps. 111
Praise the Lord!
PH 225; PPCS 111

1 Cor. 8:1–13
Though I May Speak
PH 335

Mark 1:21–28
Lord, Whose Love Through Humble Service
PH 427

Daily Lectionary
Ps. 23, 66, 108, 150
Isa. 51:9-16
Heb. 11:8-16; John 7:14-31

GHANA

Let Us Join in Prayer for:

PC(USA) People in Mission
Presbyterian Church of Ghana (PCG): young adult volunteers (YAV), community development interns, **Susan Deborah Baer**, **Dana Michelle Caraway**, **Kate Elizabeth Hartman**, **Joshua David Heikkila**; **Rev. Garvester Kelley**, West Africa Mission Enabler, PC(USA); **Wendy Marcia Kelley**, YAV site coordinator, PC(USA)

Partners/Ministries
PCG: **Rev. Sam Prempeh**, moderator, **Rev. Herbert Opong**, secretary, interchurch relations; Evangelical Presbyterian Church, Ghana (EPCG): **Rev. Dr. L. K. Buama**, moderator; Christian Council of Ghana: **Rev. Dr. Robert Aboagye-Mensah**, general secretary; Presbytery Partnerships with the PCG: Foothills Presbytery, Presbytery of Greater Atlanta (PATH), Presbytery of the James, Presbytery of Lackawanna, Presbytery of Mid-Kentucky, Presbytery of New Brunswick, Presbytery of North Puget Sound, and Salem Presbytery

PC(USA) General Assembly Staff
Rev. Peter Bower, CMD
Randy Bowman, DEDO

The Presbyterian Church of Ghana (PCG) was founded through the efforts of missionaries who arrived almost 175 years ago in what was then called the Gold Coast. As with all mission churches, it was originally characterized by receiving. However, the PCG quickly moved to being a missionary church characterized by sending and giving.

As part of an effort to understand the impact of having been a mission church and to recognize God's ministry to Africans in their unique context, the Akrofi-Christaller Memorial Centre for Mission Research and Applied Theology (ACMC) was founded in 1985 as a ministry of the PCG. The ACMC seeks to provide scholarly reflection and interpretive depth to inform and strengthen the African church in its task of Christian witness, spiritual nurture, and intellectual renewal.

The Rev. Dinah Abbey-Mensah is one of seventeen ordained women ministers of the Evangelical Presbyterian Church of Ghana.

The Evangelical Presbyterian Church of Ghana (EPCG) has a membership of 86,500 and 650 congregations and is largely centered in the southeastern part of the country. The Rev. Dinah Abbey-Mensah is one of seventeen ordained women ministers (out of a total of 174) of the EPCG. She talks about the importance of the church to Ghanaian life. "Church is a central part of the culture. Everyone hears the church bell ring at 4:30 each morning to remind them to be involved in morning devotions." When asked about the ministries of the EPCG, Ms. Abbey-Mensah replies, "Women are the backbone of the church. They have a vital ministry of outreach into the community as well as in support of one another. . . . I also really appreciate the youth. In my home congregation, they lead the first worship service every Sunday at 7:30 A.M. It is a vibrant service that is planned, led, and executed by youth. It is having a tremendous impact."

Total Area: 88,700 sq. mi. (slightly smaller than Oregon). **Population**: 19,894,014. **Languages**: English (official), African languages, including Akan, Moshi-Dagomba, Ewe, and Ga. **GDP Per Capita**: $1,900. **Literacy**: 64.5% (Male 75.9%, Female 53.5%). **Religions**: indigenous beliefs, Muslim, Christian, other. **Life Expectancy**: 57.24 years. **Human Development Index Rank**: 119.

Daily Lectionary

Ps. 9, 62, 73, 145
Isa. 51:17-23
Gal. 4:1-11; Mark 7:24-37

Scripture

For God alone my soul waits in silence; from [God] comes my salvation (Ps. 62:1).

NIGER

The PC(USA) works in Niger with partner l'Eglise Evangelique de la Republique du Niger, or the Evangelical Church of Niger (ECN). The partnership entered a new phase in 2002 when mission co-worker Thomas Johnson arrived to work in community development with the partner church.

Niger, a land-locked West African country that is 80 percent desert, is ranked as the second poorest nation in the world by the United Nations Development Program. The Christian community in Niger is tiny—comprising about one-half of one percent of the population. Despite its small size, the ECN has ambitious goals to grow through a holistic ministry that addresses the social, economic, and spiritual needs of the nation.

Thomas Johnson asks us to pray that God will guide the church in Niger in how to best present the full gospel in the midst of a harsh environment.

Total Area: 488,500 sq. mi. (slightly less than twice the size of Texas). **Population**: 10,355,156. **Languages**: French (official), Hausa, Djerma. **GDP Per Capita**: $1,000. **Literacy**: 13.6% (Male 20.9%, Female 6.6%). **Religions**: Muslim, indigenous beliefs, Christian. **Life Expectancy**: 41.59 years. **Human Development Index Rank**: 161.

RWANDA

Located near the equator at the edge of Lake Kivu, Rwanda is a small, beautiful, and largely rural country. Its pastoral appearance exists in sharp contrast to the horror of the ethnic bloodbath that took place there.

Ongoing ethnic tensions culminated in April 1994 in the genocide of 800,000 Tutsis by majority Hutus. The Tutsi rebels defeated the Hutu regime and ended the killing in July 1994, but approximately two million Hutu refugees fled to neighboring countries. Although most of the refugees have returned to Rwanda, the country continues to struggle with reconciliation.

Mission co-worker the Rev. Dr. Michael Parker is teaching at Faculté de Théologie Protestante de Butare, a Christian seminary located in one of the places where the genocide was most ruthlessly carried out. Forming Christian leaders who will work to bind up the wounds of the past through the gospel ministry is the most immediate task before the college.

Total Area: 9,600 sq. mi. (slightly smaller than Maryland). **Population**: 7,312,756. **Languages**: Kinyarwanda (official), French (official), English (official), Kiswahili. **GDP Per Capita**: $900. **Literacy**: 48% (Male 52%, Female 45%). **Religions**: Roman Catholic, Protestant, Adventist, Muslim, indigenous beliefs, other, none. **Life Expectancy**: 38.99 years. **Human Development Index Rank**: 152.

Scripture

How beautiful upon the mountains are the feet of the messenger who announces peace, who brings good news, who announces salvation, who says to Zion, "Your God reigns" (Isa. 52:7).

Let Us Join in Prayer for:

PC(USA) People in Mission
Thomas Richard Johnson, development worker, Evangelical Church of the Republic of Niger; **Michael Thomas Parker**, church history professor, Presbyterian Church of Rwanda

Partners/Ministries
Evangelical Church of Niger (ECN): **Rev. Hassane dan Karami**, general secretary; Presbyterian Church of Rwanda: **Rev. Dr. Elisee Musamakwele**, president; Protestant Council of Rwanda: **Rev. Richard Murigande**, general secretary; Church World Action [Rwanda]: **Mary Balikungeri**, director; Butare Theological College [Rwanda]

PC(USA) General Assembly Staff
Suzanne Bowman, FDN
Nancy Boxman, BOP
Daniel Braden, PPC

Daily Lectionary
Ps. 7, 12, 36, 146
Isa. 52:1-12
Gal. 4:12-20; Mark 8:1-10

Let Us Join in Prayer for:

Partners/Ministries
Presbyterian Church of Nigeria (PCN):
Dr. Benebo Fubara Fubara-Manuel,
principal clerk; Nigeria Christian Council:
Rev. Ubon Bassey Usung, general
secretary; Theological College of Northern
Nigeria, Jos

PC(USA) General Assembly Staff
Rev. Leah Ellison Bradley, PW
Regina Bradley, FDN
Jerry Bradshaw, MSS

NIGERIA

There has been a Presbyterian presence in Nigeria since 1846 when a Church of Scotland minister came from Jamaica. About a century later, in 1954, the Presbyterian Church of Nigeria (PCN) became autonomous. Although a minority denomination in Nigeria—only one-tenth of 1 percent—the PCN is full of committed people who are making a difference.

photo by Doug Welch

Nene Amogu and her husband, Ukagha, are among the faithful lay workers of the Presbyterian Church of Nigeria.

Nene Amogu and her husband, Ukagha, are a dynamic force in the life of the PCN congregation in Abuja. Their mission serves to stimulate the denomination to be a more outward-looking church. One of Nene's ministries continues a campaign to bring women of the PC(USA) and the PCN together to celebrate their oneness in Christ.

The Very Rev. Dr. James U. Ukaegbu, the National Director of Mission for the PCN and an unflagging evangelist, retired in 2001 from church office at age sixty. He sees himself as retiring not from active service, not from missions, but to devote himself to discipleship and mentoring to strengthen the church's pastors.

Friday Inya left a well-paying government job to serve the church full time as a pastor. In Nigeria this would be a courageous decision under any circumstances, but in Jos, where Friday lives, a pastor is automatically at the forefront of the tensions between Christians and Muslims.

In a predominantly Muslim land, the mission of the Presbyterian Church of Nigeria is described by the Very Rev. Dr. Ukaegbu as "Christianity at its best, a religion on the march, an experience that thrives best on the highway and not in the closet."

Total Area: 351,200 sq. mi. (slightly more than twice the size of California). **Population**: 126,635,626. **Languages**: English (official), Hausa, Yoruba, Igbo, Fulani. **GDP Per Capita**: $950. **Literacy**: 57.1% (Male 67.3%, Female 47.3%). **Religions**: Muslim, Christian, indigenous beliefs. **Life Expectancy**: 51.07 years. **Human Development Index Rank**: 136.

Daily Lectionary

Ps. 96, 132, 134, 147:1-11
Isa. 52:13–53:12
Gal. 4:21-31; Mark 8:11-26

Scripture

[Jesus] sighed deeply in his spirit and said, "Why does this generation ask for a sign? Truly I tell you, no sign will be given to this generation" (Mark 8:12).

SUDAN

"Our presbytery partnership has forced powerful challenges to our complacent faith," writes the Rev. David Dawson, executive presbyter of the Presbytery of Shenango, of its partnership with the Sudan Presbyterian Evangelical Church. Shenango is one of over one hundred presbyteries in the PC(USA) that have made a long-term commitment to an overseas partner to walk together in each other's faith experiences. David shares some of the challenges that have emerged with continued exposure to the Christians in the Sudan.

- Pastors in the Sudan serve ten or more churches. Responsibility for preaching, worship leadership, praying for the sick, and helping the hungry find food routinely falls to the elders of the church. Occasionally the pastor visits the congregation to hear the reports of the elders and administer the Sacrament of Baptism.
- Christians in the Sudan tell their neighbors about Jesus and how trusting him has changed their lives. They even go to prisons and baptize inmates in front of their Muslim guards. Their bold witness is one reason the church in the Sudan is among the fastest growing in the world.
- Believers in the Sudan care deeply about basic education and teaching the faith. Public education is not available, so volunteers teach in the evening under trees and in makeshift shelters. There are no books, only rough chalkboards painted on a mud wall. These teachers reach out to street boys who know more about the stories of the Bible than many of our children do.

The Sudan Presbyterian Evangelical Church is based in northern Sudan and was originally a presbytery within the Synod of the Nile in Egypt. It now has six congregations and seven mission stations in the Khartoum area. One of its ministries is among the millions of destitute refugees who have been forced out of the south and west.

Scripture

For freedom Christ has set us free. Stand firm, therefore, and do not submit again to a yoke of slavery (Gal. 5:1).

Let Us Join in Prayer for:

PC(USA) People in Mission
Barry D. Almy, Sudan/Ethiopia Mission Enabler, Presbyterian Church of the Sudan; Sudan Presbyterian Evangelical Church (SPEC): **Sue Ellen Hall**, trainer of English as a second language teachers, **Elizabeth Ann McCormick**, professor of theological studies, Nile Theological College; **Haruun L. Ruun**, executive director, New Sudan Council of Churches

Partners/Ministries
Presbyterian Church of Sudan (PCOS): **Rev. John Kang Dung**, moderator, **Rev. Stephen Oyol Awow**, general secretary, **Rev. Peter Makuac Nyak**, associate moderator, **Rev. Peter Rit Riak**, executive secretary; SPEC: **Rev. Aeily Mangasha**, moderator, **Rev. Danial Hamad**, general secretary; Presbytery Partnerships: Presbytery of Shenango with SPEC; Trinity Presbytery with PCOS

PC(USA) General Assembly Staff
Rev. John R. Bradshaw, DEDO
Sarah Brailsford, WMD

Daily Lectionary

Ps. 26, 116, 130, 147:12-20
Isa. 54:1-10 (11-17)
Gal. 5:1-15; Mark 8:27–9:1

Let Us Join in Prayer for:

Partners/Ministries
Association of Christian Relief
Organizations Southern Sudan (ACROSS)
[Sudan]: **John Horton**, chairman of the
board, **Mike Wall**, projects manager;
New Sudan Council of Churches (NSCC):
Rev. Fr. Mark Kumbonyaki, chair,
Rev. Peter Tibi, deputy chairman,
Rev. Dr. Haruun Ruun, executive
secretary; Nile Theological College (NTC)
[Sudan]: **Rev. Michael Chot Lul**,
principal, **Rev. Ishmael Kanani**, dean;
Sudan Council of Churches (SCC):
Rev. Enock Tombe Stephens, general
secretary; Gereif Bible College [Sudan];
Giffen Bible College [Sudan]; Evangelical
Presbyterian Church of Togo (EEPT):
Rev. Dr. Gerson Kodzo BESSA,
moderator, **Rev. Frank Adubra**,
general secretary

PC(USA) General Assembly Staff
Ella Brazley, PPC
Dr. Dorothy Brewster-Lee, WMD
Richard Brier, DEDO

Daily Lectionary

Ps. 25, 40, 84, 148
Isa. 55:1-13
Gal. 5:16-24; Mark 9:2-13

SUDAN, *continued*

Peacemaking Ministry of the New Sudan Council of Churches

The Sudan, the largest country in Africa, has been plagued with decades of almost constant civil war. Hunger, disease, exposure, and death continue to be the norm in this conflict that has cost over two million lives and displaced over four million people.

To complicate the issue, since 1991 groups of people in southern Sudan have also been fighting one another, mostly along ethnic lines. This has made the government's task easier in fighting a divided enemy. In addition to its work among the internally displaced and in peacemaking at the community level, the New Sudan Council of Churches has worked to get the leaders of the two major factions to talk with one another. In January 2002 their efforts came to fruition when the Nairobi Declaration of Peace and Unity was signed.

Total Area: 916,300 sq. mi. (slightly more than one-quarter the size of the United States). **Population**: 36,080,373. **Languages**: Arabic (official), Nubian, Ta Bedawie, diverse dialects of Nilotic, Nilo-Hamitic, Sudanic languages, English. **GDP Per Capita**: $1,000. **Literacy**: 46.1% (Male 57.7%, Female 34.6%). **Religions**: Sunni Muslim, indigenous beliefs, Christian. **Life Expectancy**: 56.94 years. **Human Development Index Rank**: 138.

TOGO

The Evangelical Presbyterian Church of Togo (EEPT) and the Evangelical Presbyterian Church of Ghana share common roots: both are products of the German Bremen mission on the Slave Coast of what are now Ghana and Togo.

The EEPT, officially named in 1959, has 516 congregations, 300,000 members, and 71 pastors, including 12 women. The EEPT has several rural and urban centers that are responsible for the church's ministries in the areas of health, agriculture, and education. It is active in the health and welfare of the country, running 105 primary schools, 4 secondary schools, 3 dispensaries, and a hospital.

Total Area: 21,000 sq. mi. (slightly smaller than West Virginia). **Population**: 5,153,088. **Languages**: French (official), Ewe, Mina, Kabye, Dagomba. **GDP Per Capita**: $1,500. **Literacy**: 51.7% (Male 67%, Female 37%). **Religions**: indigenous beliefs, Christian, Muslim. **Life Expectancy**: 54.35 years. **Human Development Index Rank**: 128.

Scripture

The fruit of the Spirit is love, joy, peace, patience, kindness, generosity, faithfulness, gentleness, and self-control. There is no law against such things (Gal. 5:22–23).

SOUTHERN AND EAST AFRICA

Ethiopia

Uganda

Kenya

Tanzania

Malawi

Madagascar

Angola

Zambia

Namibia

Zimbabwe

Mauritius

Botswana

Mozambique

Swaziland

South Africa

Lesotho

Let Us Join in Prayer for:

Partners/Ministries
All Africa Conference of Churches:
The Very Rev. Dr. Kwesi Dickson,
president, **Rev. Melaku Kifle**, interim
general secretary; Project for Christian-
Muslim Relations in Africa PROCMURA):
Rev. Iteffa Gobena, president,
Rev. Dr. Johnson Mbillah, general
adviser; Alliance of Reformed Churches in
Africa (ARCA): **Rev. Majaha Nhliziyo**,
coordinator; Council of Churches in
Namibia: **Venerable Nangula Evalisa
Kathindi**, general secretary; Evangelical
Lutheran Church in the Republic of
Namibia: **Rev. Gotthart Gurirab**, dean;
Christian Council of Tanzania: **Dr. Wilson
L. Mtebe**, general secretary; Evangelical
Lutheran Church in Tanzania; Ilembula
Lutheran School [Tanzania]; Mpechi
Secondary School [Tanzania]; Njombe
District Development Trust [Tanzania]

PC(USA) General Assembly Staff
Charlene Briggs, EDO
Mary Bright, PPC
Robert Britton, WMD

I n the midst of civil strife and dislocation, natural disaster and human suffering, and a maze of competing religious ideologies and claims, Christians in the Southern and Eastern regions of Africa are coming together, providing a voice for the voiceless, facilitating humanitarian assistance, and witnessing to God's love shown in the gift, sacrifice, and resurrection of Christ Jesus. Presbyterian mission personnel with a wide variety of skills and talents are vitally engaged with our African church partners and the ecumenical community in this ministry.

Scripture
Thus says the LORD: Maintain justice, and do what is right, for soon my salvation will come, and my deliverance be revealed (Isa. 56:1).

Daily Lectionary
Ps. 63, 90, 125, 149
Isa. 56:1-8
Gal. 5:25–6:10; Mark 9:14-29

Sunday Lectionary and Hymns

Isa. 40:21–31
God Created Heaven and Earth
PH 290

Ps. 147:1–11, 20c
When the Morning Stars Together
PH 486; PPCS 153

1 Cor. 9:16–23
Today We All Are Called to Be Disciples
PH 434

Mark 1:29–39
Live Into Hope
PH 332

THE LORD'S DAY

MINUTE FOR MISSION
THE CHURCH AND THE CRIMINAL JUSTICE SYSTEM

Paul's first letter to the church in Corinth includes these words: "To those outside the law I became as one outside the law (though I am not free from God's law but am under Christ's law) so that I might win those outside the law. To the weak I became weak, so that I might win the weak. . . . I do it all for the sake of the gospel, so that I may share in its blessings" (1 Cor. 9:21–23).

The Rev. Marla Cates is the embodiment of Paul's declaration. Winner of the Presbyterian Church (U.S.A.) Restorative Justice Award for 2002, Marla serves as chaplain in the North Carolina Correctional Center for Women in Raleigh. As Christ identifies with us in our own weakness, her encounters with women who have been declared "outside the law" involve a measure of identification. Marla becomes a symbol of caring and hope to those women as they begin to recognize that one day they may be restored to society and to their loved ones.

> *At the heart of the commitment of the Presbyterian Church (U.S.A.) to restorative justice is the threefold commitment to the restoration of the victim, the offender, and the community.*

In addition to her duties as chaplain, Marla coordinates the work of the Presbyterian Chaplaincy Coordinating Committee, through which numerous volunteer mentors are recruited from area churches for ministry to prisoners. They focus on women who are eligible for release within five years, providing prerelease planning and training and support after they are released. As a result of this ministry, many women reenter society as productive citizens and in the process reduce the high level of recidivism that plagues our criminal justice system.

At the heart of the commitment of the Presbyterian Church (U.S.A.) to restorative justice is the threefold commitment to the restoration of the victim, the offender, and the community. Because of the ministry of the Rev. Marla Cates and those who work with her, such restoration becomes a living reality.

—*Rev. Vernon S. Broyles III, associate director, Social Justice*

Prayer
God of grace, we know that we are the recipients of your forgiving love day after day, year after year. As we seek ways to be faithful to Jesus' command to visit those who are in prison, challenge us to new and more active ministries to those whom our society has declared "outside the law," that they may know through us the restorative love of Jesus Christ. In Jesus' name we pray. Amen.

Daily Lectionary

Ps. 103, 117, 139, 150
Isa. 57:1-13
Heb. 12:1-6; John 7:37-46

SOUTHERN AND EAST AFRICA

continued

From Ethiopia to South Africa, God is pouring out the Holy Spirit, empowering mission throughout the continent. In Zimbabwe, in spite of political instability, food shortages, and a faltering economy, the church is still in the business of saving body, mind, and spirit. Max T. Chiguida, moderator of the General Assembly of the Uniting Presbyterian Church of Southern Africa, writes, "Like salt, the Presbyterian Church in Zimbabwe's work and witness have given glory to God, and the salt has not lost its taste" (Matt. 5:13). A PC(USA) partner organization, Back to God Ministry, was asked by the Anglican Church of Uganda to conduct HIV/AIDS awareness campaigns in all of the dioceses. It became part of Uganda's tremendous success story in lowering the country's HIV infection rates. In South Africa, PC(USA) mission co-worker Cindy Easterday, who works with African Enterprise ministries, is helping to link churches across racial lines as part of a creative strategy for HIV/AIDS awareness education. The South Africa Council of Churches is actively involved in providing food, warm clothing, and blankets during natural disasters. In Lesotho, mission co-worker Bob Franklin is the facilitator of the Joining Hands Against Hunger program. He coordinates efforts among various groups involved in both South Africa and neighboring countries—Botswana, Malawi, and Mozambique—in the struggle against hunger and poverty.

Amidst all the strife and hardship in the region, the growth of the church continues. The Ethiopian Evangelical Church Mekane Yesus, a denomination of almost 5 million members, has experienced a 15 percent annual growth rate for several years. One of the smallest denominations in the region, the Presbyterian Church of Mauritius, has developed a cell group ministry that has seen some congregations grow as much as 250 percent in the past five years.

As you read the stories in this *Mission Yearbook for Prayer & Study* about people in Southern and East Africa who, against incredible odds have responded with deep faith and commitment to God's call in their lives, we hope you will be inspired and moved to watch, work, and pray for Africa.

—*Rev. Jon T. Chapman, coordinator, Southern and East Africa*

Let Us Join in Prayer for:

Partners/Ministries
Christian Organizations Research Advisory Trust [Kenya]: **Margaret W. Mwaura**, executive director; Daystar University [Kenya]; National Christian Council of Kenya: **Rev. Mutava Musyimi**, general secretary; Pastoral Training Institute [Kenya]: **Rev. Dr. Plawson Kuria**, principal; St. Paul's Theological College [Kenya]

PC(USA) General Assembly Staff
Sherry Britton, NMD
Elder Mindy Broad, BOP
Mamie Broadhurst, NMD

Daily Lectionary
Ps. 5, 29, 82, 145
Isa. 57:14-21
Gal. 6:11-18; Mark 9:30-41

Scripture
May the LORD give strength to his people! May the LORD bless his people with peace! (Ps. 29:11).

Let Us Join in Prayer for:

Partners/Ministries
Christian Council [Botswana]:
David Modiega, general secretary;
Western Wollega Bethel Synod [Ethiopia]:
Rev. Teferi Barkessa, president; Bethel
Mekane Yesus School [Ethiopia];
Mekane Yesus Seminary [Ethiopia]:
Rev. Dr. Debela Birri, principal; Western
Gambela Bethel Synod [Ethiopia]:
Rev. David Thoak, president; Illubabor
Bethel Synod [Ethiopia]: **Ato Yonas
Yigezu, Namibia** president

PC(USA) General Assembly Staff
Elder Alice Broadwater, EDO
William Brock, OGA
Charlotte Brooks, OGA

Daily Lectionary

Ps. 42, 102, 133, 146
Isa. 58:1-12
2 Tim. 1:1-14; Mark 9:42-50

BOTSWANA

Fueled by diamond mining and sales, Botswana has maintained one of the world's highest rates of economic expansion since becoming independent. Although the standard of living has improved, Botswana's rate of HIV/AIDS infection is among the highest in the world.

The PC(USA) relates to churches in Botswana through its partner relationship with the Botswana Christian Council. Also located in Botswana is the headquarters of the Alliance of Reformed Churches in Africa (ARCA). The Rev. Majaha Nhlizigo of ARCA writes, "Being in a region of the world most affected by HIV/AIDS, we have made this ministry a priority. As we heed our calling to mission, we invite sisters and brothers in the Reformed faith all around the world to be partners in our mission challenge."

Total Area: 225,700 sq. mi. (slightly smaller than Texas). **Population**: 1,586,119. **Languages**: English (official), Setswana. **GDP Per Capita**: $6,600. **Literacy**: 69.8% (Male 80.5%, Female 59.9%). **Religions**: indigenous beliefs, Christian. **Life Expectancy**: 37.13 years. **Human Development Index Rank**: 114.

ETHIOPIA

The Ethiopian Evangelical Church Mekane Yesus (EECMY), the PC(USA) partner in Ethiopia, attempts to meet the many needs of the country's people. Church members feed the hungry and provide health care services, child and youth programs, special schools for the physically challenged, HIV/AIDS control and prevention programs, educational activities, water development programs, rehabilitative rural development programs, and evangelism.

In spite of the harsh day-to-day struggle of the Ethiopian people, the EECMY has experienced a 15 percent growth rate each year for many years. This phenomenal growth is both miraculous and challenging as the church struggles to provide effective ministry with very limited resources. The church has a very deliberate twofold witness to the gospel of Jesus Christ, in word and deed, and the needs of people are primary in the midst of evangelizing and building hundreds of new church buildings.

Total Area: 431,800 sq. mi. (slightly less than twice the size of Texas). **Population**: 65,891,874. **Languages**: Amharic, Tigrinya, Orominga, Guaragigna, Somali, Arabic, English. **GDP Per Capita**: $600. **Literacy**: 35.5% (Male 45.5%, Female 25.3%). **Religions**: Muslim, Ethiopian Orthodox, animist, other. **Life Expectancy**: 44.68 years. **Human Development Index Rank**: 158.

Scripture

Is not this the fast that I choose: to loose the bonds of injustice, to undo the thongs of the yoke, to let the oppressed go free, and to break every yoke? (Isa. 58:6).

ETHIOPIA, *continued*

And Then the Rains Came

PC(USA) mission co-workers John and Gwenyth Haspels work in southwestern Ethiopia at the invitation of the Ethiopian Evangelical Church Mekane Yesus. They work and live among the Surma, a seminomadic tribe numbering about 30,000, on a comprehensive program that includes evangelism, education, medical care, and development work.

A young Surma girl smiles after having been vaccinated.

The Haspels share this story of an answer to prayer that halted a meningitis epidemic. "In mid-February during our regular Friday night prayer time, prayer was requested for rain in order to slow down and stop the spread of meningitis. Because many parts of Ethiopia were affected by the epidemic, we were informed that no vaccines were available for us because priority was given to areas with larger populations.

"On Saturday afternoon, an emergency team of medical workers and a doctor arrived with vaccine and drugs. As they sat in our living room, it started to rain. The medical officer in charge, shouting over the noise of the rain on the tin roof, said, 'You know, don't you, that this rain can do more than all our efforts combined to put a stop to this epidemic.' We sat there praising God for the provision not only of the drugs and vaccines, which were needed, but also for the rain and for additional personnel to help in giving vaccinations. Normally February is our driest month of the year, with little or no rain. We had three inches of rain in two days, which even in the rainy season would be considered a big rain. The epidemic has been contained."

The Haspels ask for prayer for the Surma church and for wisdom as they prepare a three-year proposal to the Ethiopian government for their continued work in this region.

Scripture
[Jesus] said to them, "Let the little children come to me; do not stop them; for it is to such as these that the kingdom of God belongs" (Mark 10:14).

Let Us Join in Prayer for:

PC(USA) People in Mission
Ethiopian Evangelical Church Mekane Yesus (EECMY): **Gwenyth Ellen Adair Haspels**, nurse, **Rev. John Mark Haspels**, evangelist, **Marie Annette Lusted**, nurse/translator; Western Wollega Synod: **Rev. Michael Scott Weller**, evangelist, **Rachel Elizabeth Weller**, team ministry; **Jo Ann Griffith**, teacher, Bethel Evangelical Secondary School (BESS)

Partners/Ministries
EECMY: **Rev. Iteffa Gobena**, president, **Ato Solomon Nega,** Bethel Synods Coordination Office, coordinator; Bethel Evangelical Secondary School (BESS): **Ato Asefa Ayana**, director; Berhane Yesus Elementary School: **Ato Thomas Nano**, president; Eastern Gambella Bethel Synod: **Ato Omat Agwa**, president; Southwest Bethel Synod: **Rev. Yohannes Sherab**, president; Presbytery Partnerships with the EECMY: Presbytery of Shenandoah, Presbytery of Susquehanna Valley, and Washington Presbytery

PC(USA) General Assembly Staff
Sammie Brooks, MSS
Leanne Brower, NMD

Daily Lectionary
Ps. 1, 33, 89:1-18, 147:1-11
Isa. 59:1-21
2 Tim 1:15–2:13; Mark 10:1-16

Let Us Join in Prayer for:

PC(USA) People in Mission
Ruth L. Montgomery, mission volunteer, primary school teacher, Back to God Evangelistic Association [Uganda]; **Robert Karl Franklin**, companionship facilitator [Lesotho]; **Samantha E. Thompson-Franklin**, librarian, Lesotho Evangelical Church (LEC)

Partners/Ministries
LEC: **Rev. John R. Mokhalane**, president, **Rev. T. S. Lentsoenyane**, executive secretary; Lay Training Center Women's Training Program [Lesotho]: **E. Tiheli**, LEC education secretary; Morija Ecumenical Conference and Training Center [Lesotho]; Morija Theological Seminary [Lesotho]: **Rev. Dr. A. M. Moseme**, director

PC(USA) General Assembly Staff
Bonnie Brown, MSS
Brian Brown, FDN
Cora Brown, DEDO
Diane Brown, BOP

Daily Lectionary

Ps. 16, 62, 97, 147:12-20
Isa. 60:1-22
2 Tim. 2:14-26; Mark 10:17-31

UGANDA

Uganda, in contrast to the trend in sub-Saharan Africa, has lowered its HIV infection rates. This success has been brought about by an extensive partnership in all sectors of a society that has a high commitment to HIV education and prevention.

Peterson Sozi, executive director and founder of the Back to God (BTG) ministry, writes that BTG began incorporating HIV/AIDS awareness campaigns in its evangelistic outreach in 1987. Although a predominantly Presbyterian organization, BTG was asked by the Anglican Church of Uganda, in which over 35 percent of the Ugandan population are members, to expand the program to all of its dioceses.

One by-product of the disease has been a large increase in the number of children needing primary education who cannot afford to pay for it. Mission co-worker Ruth Montgomery is part of a BTG ministry addressing this need through her teaching at the Mwera School.

Total Area: 77,000 sq. mi. (slightly smaller than Oregon). **Population**: 23,985,712. **Languages**: English (official), Ganda or Luganda, other Niger-Congo languages, Nilo-Saharan languages, Swahili, Arabic. **GDP Per Capita**: $1,100. **Literacy**: 61.8% (Male 73.7%, Female 50.2%). **Religions**: Roman Catholic, Protestant, Muslim, indigenous beliefs. **Life Expectancy**: 43.37 years. **Human Development Index Rank**: 141.

LESOTHO

Mission co-workers Samantha and Bob Franklin serve in Lesotho at the invitation of the PC(USA)'s partner, the Lesotho Evangelical Church. Samantha works at the library of the Koapeng Theological Seminary in Morija. The seminary, run by the Lesotho Evangelical Church, prepares African students for full-time ministry.

Bob is a facilitator in a pilot program of the Presbyterian Hunger Program called Joining Hands Against Hunger (JHAH) which helps to coordinate effort among groups involved in the struggle against hunger and poverty. JHAH addresses the impact of globalization on local and national economies and engages governments and corporations to consider how their policies affect the poor. Another aim is to partner with U.S. churches in these efforts.

Total Area: 11,700 sq. mi. (slightly smaller than Maryland). **Population**: 2,177,062. **Languages**: Sesotho (southern Sotho), English (official), Zulu, Xhosa. **GDP Per Capita**: $2,400. **Literacy**: 83% (Male 72%, Female 93%). **Religions**: Christian, indigenous beliefs. **Life Expectancy**: 48.84 years. **Human Development Index Rank**: 120.

Scripture

Jesus, looking at him, loved him and said, "You lack one thing; go, sell what you own, and give the money to the poor, and you will have treasure in heaven; then come, follow me" (Mark 10:21).

KENYA

"Kenya is one of the few remaining places where one can still get a sense of the fullness of God's original creation," writes PC(USA) mission co-worker Silvia Wilson. "On closer inspection, however, one will find that all is not well in paradise."

The number of orphans is rising due to a host of factors, including the HIV/AIDS epidemic. The economy is stagnating because of poor management and uneven commitment to reform. Deforestation and pollution overwhelm the environment. Ethnic clashes destabilize communities, and increasing numbers of people continue to be thrust into poverty. Natural and human resources are being stretched to the limit.

With support from overseas partners, the Presbyterian Church of East Africa (PCEA) is having an impact on these problems. Water conservation and tree planting programs have been implemented. Homes have been built for orphans. Assistance is now available for displaced communities and others in crisis. "Such activities would be commendable under any circumstances. When we remember that the PCEA has only 600 trained pastors and evangelists to serve thousands of congregations and millions of members, their accomplishments are an awesome testimony to the presence of the Creator and the power of partnership," reports Silvia.

Presbyterian Teachers College-Rubate, a teacher-training college located in a rural area of the central highlands, is part of the educational ministry of the PCEA. PC(USA) mission volunteer Marion Strain has witnessed the life-changing experience the college can give its students. She writes, "During the years I have taught and lived at Rubate I have seen the college give students hope and an aim in life to use and develop the potential that they can be a living witness for Jesus Christ."

Total Area: 219,500 sq. mi. (slightly more than twice the size of Nevada). **Population**: 30,765,916. **Languages**: English and Kiswahili (official), numerous indigenous languages. **GDP Per Capita**: $1,500. **Literacy**: 78.1% (Male 86.3%, Female 70%). **Religions**: Protestant, Roman Catholic, indigenous beliefs, Muslim, other. **Life Expectancy**: 47.49 years. **Human Development Index Rank**: 123.

Scripture
The sacrifice acceptable to God is a broken spirit; a broken and contrite heart, O God, you will not despise (Ps. 51:17).

Let Us Join in Prayer for:

PC(USA) People in Mission
Presbyterian Church of East Africa (PCEA): **Rev. Dr. Marta Dawn Bennett**, professor (senior lecturer), Daystar University, **Irma de la Torre**, nurse, **Dr. Salvador de la Torre**, community health program facilitator, **Sue Anne Fairman**, team ministry, Daystar University, **Rev. Timothy Joseph Fairman**, student ministries, Daystar University, **Marion L. Strain**, mission volunteer, English teacher, **Dr. Ane Mia Topple**, mission volunteer, dermatologist, **Dr. Stanley Craig Topple**, mission volunteer, physician; Young Adult Volunteer, Community Development Interns, PCEA: **Marta Sann Johnson**, **Michelle Lynn Rasmussen**, **Ryan David Rasmussen**, and **Jonathan Allen Warren**; Rift Valley Academy: **James Jay Long**, superintendent, **Kathleen Belle Long**, administrative assistant; Presbytery Partnerships with the PCEA: Presbytery of Blackhawk, Cimarron Presbytery, Presbytery of Detroit, Presbytery of Los Ranchos, National Capital Presbytery, Presbytery of Newton, Presbytery of the Redwoods, and the Presbytery of West Virginia

Partners/Ministries
PCEA: **Rt. Rev. Dr. Jesse M. Kamau**, moderator, **Rev. Patrick M. Rukenya**, general secretary

PC(USA) General Assembly Staff
Frances M. Brown, PW

Daily Lectionary
Ps. 51, 65, 142, 148
Isa. 61:1-9
2 Tim. 3:1-17; Mark 10:32-45

MADAGASCAR

Let Us Join in Prayer for:

PC(USA) People in Mission
Church of Jesus Christ in Madagascar
(FJKM): **Dr. Joanne E. Brown**, professor
of theology, **Rev. Cynthia Holder-Rich**,
lecturer in theology, **Elizabeth Warlick
Turk**, public health specialist,
Development Office, **Robert Daniell
Turk**, forestry environmental specialist,
Development Office

Partners/Ministries
FJKM: **Rev. Edmond Razafimahefa**,
president, **Rev. Lilia Rafalimanana**,
vice president, **Andrianary Rasomoela**,
vice president, **Rev. Charles
Rakondrakamana**, general secretary,
Jean Emmanuel D'Elnivo, director,
Evangelism and Mission Department;
Akany Avoko Remand Home for Girls;
Faculté of Theology at Antananarivo;
Seminary at Ivatos; Presbytery Partnership
with the FJKM: Synod of the Northeast

PC(USA) General Assembly Staff
James Brown, BOP
Kelly Brown, BOP
Patricia Brown, NMD

The giant island nation of Madagascar was in turmoil after the disputed election of December 2001. Supporters of Marc Ravalomanana, businessperson and vice president of the Church of Jesus Christ in Madagascar (FJKM)—the PC(USA) partner church in Madagascar—insisted he won 52 percent of votes cast. The High Constitutional Court, however, ruled that he won just over 46 percent and had to face President Didier Ratsiraka in a runoff election. Ravalomanana's supporters suspected Raksiraka of massive election fraud in the election and had no confidence that a runoff election would be handled any differently.

In February 2002, after strikes and demonstrations against President Ratsiraka, Mr. Ravalomanana's supporters inaugurated him as president in Antananarivo, the capital. Mission co-worker Cynthia Holder-Rich writes about the event. "After suffering since 1975 under Ratsiraka and seeing development disappear, the people, who felt they had already elected a new president, simply would not accept anything less than the inauguration of the man they chose. This inauguration took place in front of hundreds of thousands of supporters, the highest judges in the land and the leaders of all four major Christian churches in the country, including Ravalomanana's own church."

Mr. Ratsiraka, the country's leader for many of the last twenty-five years, clung to the presidency and set up an alternative capital in the port city of Toamasina.

In Madagascar, one of the world's poorest and least developed countries, life has always been difficult, and having two presidents did not make it any easier. With no one entirely in charge, the country's fragile economy suffered. While there are signs that the contested presidency is now firmly in the hands of Marc Ravalomanana, Madagascar has lost valuable ground in its struggle against poverty and deprivation.

Total Area: 224,300 sq. mi. (slightly less than twice the size of Arizona). **Population**: 15,982,563. **Languages**: French and Malagasy (official). **GDP Per Capita**: $800. **Literacy**: 80% (Male 88%, Female 73%). **Religions**: indigenous beliefs, Christian, Muslim. **Life Expectancy**: 55.35 years. **Human Development Index Rank**: 135.

Daily Lectionary

Ps. 98, 104, 138, 149
Isa. 61:10–62:5
2 Tim. 4:1-8; Mark 10:46-52

Scripture
I have fought the good fight, I have finished the race, I have kept the faith (2 Tim. 4:7).

THE LORD'S DAY

MINUTE FOR MISSION
AUSTIN PRESBYTERIAN THEOLOGICAL SEMINARY

**Sunday Lectionary
and Hymns**

2 Kings 5:1–14
Out of Deep, Unordered Water
PH 494

Ps. 30
Come Sing to God
PH 181; PPCS 27

1 Cor. 9:24–27
Guide My Feet
PH 354

Mark 1:40–45
Creating God, Your Fingers Trace
PH 134

I n his forty-two years as a pastor, Austin Seminary alumnus Phineas Washer earned a reputation as a peacemaker. Now retired, Washer has found a new calling: the campaign to ban land mines.

According to UNICEF, there are 110 million mines buried in sixty-four countries worldwide. These weapons—some left over from long-ended conflicts—kill more than eight hundred people a month and maim thousands more. Most victims are civilians; many are children. Since 1997, 142 nations have signed the Mine Ban Treaty, but the United States is not among them.

Phineas Washer learned of the movement when he read an article written by former UN Secretary-General Boutros Boutros-Ghali. He subsequently has attended national conferences, participated in a congressional briefing, and lobbied legislators. During that time, Washer reports, nine members of Congress have moved on the issue. Washer also authored an overture to the 2002 General Assembly urging the United States to comply with the 1997 Mine Ban Treaty.

In 2001, the Austin Seminary Association honored Washer with its Award for Service, citing his contributions to the church and his tireless efforts for peace. We are grateful that Phineas Washer continues to sow seeds of peace in landscapes scarred by violence.

Austin Seminary alumnus Phineas Washer (left), recipient of the Award for Service, is pictured with fellow award recipient Michael Murray.

—*David Gambrell, associate for public relations,*
Austin Presbyterian Theological Seminary

Prayer
O God of love and peace, grant us wisdom and resolve to make this, your world, a safe place for all your children. Deliver us from the ways that diminish and destroy life and lead us into the paths that enrich and fulfill life. Through Jesus Christ our Lord. Amen.

Daily Lectionary
Ps. 19, 81, 113, 150
Isa. 62:6-12
1 John 2:3-11; John 8:12-19

Let Us Join in Prayer for:

PC(USA) People in Mission
Church of Central Africa Presbyterian
(CCAP): **Rev. Deborah Ann Chase**,
clergy advisor to synod on women's issues,
Livingstonia Synod, **Frank Eugene
Dimmock**, coordinator, CCAP health
programs, Southern Africa Regional health
consultant, **Nancy Miller Dimmock**,
community hospitality, **Dorothy Hanson**,
mission volunteer, RN, midwife, **Dr. Mary
Sue Makin**, medical doctor, Synod of
Zimbabwe, **James William McGill**, water
specialist and construction consultant,
Jodi Jean McGill, public health worker,
Martha Anne Sommers, medical officer
and surgeon

PC(USA) General Assembly Staff
Rose Brown, BOP
Sondra Brown, BOP
Thomas Browne, NMD

Daily Lectionary

Ps. 97, 112, 135, 145
Isa. 63:1-6
1 Tim. 1:1-17; Mark 11:1-11

MALAWI

photo by: Dody Crowell

*Veronica Matinga winnowing
soya at Domasi Mission.*

Several mission workers from Malawi have
written about lessons they have learned from
the Malawian people with whom they live and
work. Mission co-workers Jennifer and Scott
Rodehaver share some observations about the
differences in attitudes of westerners and
Malawians. "There is a community we see in our
Malawian friends that goes very deep. They sacrifice
constantly for one another and do this without any
show of self-pity or complaining. My friend the
Rev. Jeremiah Chienda says, 'You westerners keep
time; in Malawi we take time.' In other words, let
us be together instead of watching the clock to
make sure we are on schedule. I am not suggesting
we are wrong in the way we deal with time or community, but rather that we
should look at how we live and see if there are different ways of relating that are
more enriching, more significant, and more Christ-like."

Former mission co-worker Dody Crowell also writes about the generous spirit of
Malawians at Domasi Mission. "Just as in Biblical times, all planting and harvesting
are done by hand. Many hours are spent preparing the fields, sowing, threshing,
winnowing, husking, and pounding to provide food for the family. Sixty-five
percent of the population lives in poverty, and during the rainy season these people
are hungry. Yet at harvest time, the women proceed to the front of the church with
baskets, bundles, and basins on their heads containing the fruits of their harvest.
There is much joy and singing as they place these items in front of the Communion
Table as an act of thanksgiving for the blessings that God has bestowed on them. It
is a colorful and heartfelt ceremony whose participants share what little they have
with the church and to the glory of God."

Total Area: 36,300 sq. mi. (slightly smaller than Pennsylvania). **Population**: 10,548,250. **Languages**:
English and Chichewa (official), other languages important regionally. **GDP Per Capita**: $900. **Literacy**:
58% (Male 72.8%, Female 43.4%). **Religions**: Protestant, Roman Catholic, Muslim, indigenous beliefs.
Life Expectancy: 37.08 years. **Human Development Index Rank**: 151.

Scripture
*Praise the LORD, for the LORD is good; sing to [the Lord's] name, for [the Lord] is
gracious (Ps. 135:3).*

MALAWI

"Fill Malawi's Basket with Food! We Have Some to Share"

In April 2002, Presbyterian Disaster Assistance provided $200,000 (primarily from One Great Hour of Sharing funds) in response to the widespread famine in which 70 percent of Malawi's ten million inhabitants risk starvation. "The findings in the visit to the project areas were astonishing," said PDA relief specialist Hudson Lugano. "I found myself weeping as I faced the severity of the need." Despite the incredible hardship faced by the people, powerful stories have emerged of how God is providing, such as one told by the Rev. Gene Straatmeyer, a PC(USA) pastor serving in Lilongwe.

A Christian Malawian family was hungry. The baby was crying for food. The mother decided to pray with her husband that God would help them. Though the husband was skeptical, they prayed for God's help. After praying nothing changed. There were a couple of ears of maize on the table. That was it. So the mother took her biggest basket and put the two ears of maize in it. She didn't go to the usual mill where she ground

The feeding program in Matapila is part of the church's response to hunger.

corn because she was ashamed that she didn't have food. So she walked to a distant mill. When it was her turn to have her corn ground, the mill manager asked her why she carried such a large basket on her head for just two ears of maize. She said it was because she was ashamed and didn't want others to know she had so little. A woman who was having her maize ground heard the conversation and said to the manager, "Fill her basket full of flour! I have some to share." The mother shouted as loudly as she could, "Praise the Lord!"

Scripture
"So I tell you, whatever you ask for in prayer, believe that you have received it, and it will be yours" (Mark 11:24).

Let Us Join in Prayer for:

Partners/Ministries
Church of Central Africa Presbyterian (CCAP)—Blantyre Synod: **Rev. Daniel Gunya**, general secretary, **Rev. Greyson Mputeni**, deputy general secretary; General Synod: **Rev. Y. A. Chienda**, senior clerk; Henry Henderson Institute Secondary School; Livingstonia Synod: **Rev. Howard Matiya Nkhoma**, general secretary, **Rev. Ted Mwambila**, deputy general secretary; Nkhoma Synod: **Rev. Dr. Winston R. Kawale**, general secretary; Embangweni, Mulanje, Ekwendeni, David Gordon, and Nkhoma hospitals; Malawi Council of Churches: **Rev. Dr. A. C. Musopole**, general secretary; Zomba Theological College (ZTC): **Dr. D. S. Mwakanandi**, principal, **Rev. Dr. Saindi Chipangwe**, vice principal; Private Hospital Association of Malawi; Robert Laws Secondary School; Presbytery Partnerships with the CCAP: Presbytery of Eastern Oklahoma, Presbytery of Northern New York, and Pittsburgh Presbytery

PC(USA) General Assembly Staff
Rev. William Browne, WMD
Rev. Vernon Broyles, NMD
Deborah Bruce, EDO

Daily Lectionary
Ps. 30, 86, 123, 146
Isa. 63:7-14
1 Tim. 1:18–2:8 (9-15); Mark 11:12-26

Let Us Join in Prayer for:

Partners/Ministries

Presbyterian Church of Mauritius:
Rev. Rodney Curpanen, moderator;
South African Council of Churches:
Rev. Dr. Molefe Tsele, general secretary;
Theological School at Fort Hare University
[South Africa]; Presbytery Partnerships
[South Africa]: Presbytery of Donegal,
Presbytery of Florida, Presbytery of New
York City, North Alabama Presbytery,
Presbytery of Northern New England with
the Uniting Presbyterian Church in
Southern Africa; Presbytery of Western
New York with the Uniting Reformed
Church in Southern Africa; Presbytery of
Western Reserve with the CLEVESA
(Cleveland-South Africa)

PC(USA) General Assembly Staff
Michelle Bruce, DEDO
Cathy Bruner, DEDO
Laura Bryan, NMD

Daily Lectionary

Ps. 4, 15, 48, 147:1-11
Isa. 63:15–64:9
1 Tim. 3:1-16; Mark 11:27–12:12

MAURITIUS

The Presbyterian Church of Mauritius (PCM), PC(USA)'s partner denomination in Mauritius, has only five congregations, but it is growing. The Rev. Rodney Curpanen, the moderator of the PCM, is both general secretary for the church and the pastor of the English-speaking congregation at St. Columba. He has a strong desire for evangelism to have a central place in the PCM. His church has cell groups that provide nurture as well as leadership and evangelism training. The Rev. France Cangy, who pastors the St. Joseph congregation in Grand Gaube, also has a strong cell-group ministry, and the church has grown 250 percent in the past five years. Mission co-workers Bob and Bobbi Snyder ask us to pray for the leadership of the PCM, the strengthening of its outreach ministries, the raising up of new pastors, and the spread of cell groups.

Total Area: 700 sq. mi. (almost 11 times the size of Washington, D.C.). **Population**: 1,189,825. **Languages**: English (official), Creole, French, Hindi, Urdu, Hakka, Bojpoori. **GDP Per Capita**: $10,400. **Literacy**: 82.9% (Male 87.1%, Female 78.8%). **Religions**: Hindu, Christian, Muslim, other. **Life Expectancy**: 71.25 years. **Human Development Index Rank**: 63.

REPUBLIC OF SOUTH AFRICA

Mission co-worker Douglas J. Tilton works with a PC(USA) partner organization, the South African Council of Churches (SACC), in its Public Policy Office. During the winter of 2001, Douglas participated in the SACC's emergency relief response to the flooding that devastated the poorest communities of Cape Town.

"The SACC acted rapidly, with the assistance of international church relief agencies, to supply food, warm clothing, and blankets. One weekend we used a meat truck to move more than five tons of blankets to a community called Wallacedene. Just getting the truck close to the distribution point was a major operation involving narrow roads, a forked stick to lift power cables high enough for the truck to pass . . . and lots of mud. The experience made me appreciate the holistic nature of the SACC's program. The Council is working to make immediate and concrete contributions to improving people's lives."

Total Area: 470,900 sq. mi. (slightly less than twice the size of Texas). **Population**: 43,586,097. **Languages**: 11 official languages, including Afrikaans, English, Ndebele, Pedi, Sotho, Swazi, Tsonga, Tswana, Venda, Xhosa, and Zulu. **GDP Per Capita**: $8,500. **Literacy**: 81.8% (Male 81.9%, Female 81.7%). **Religions**: Christian, Muslim, Hindu, indigenous and animistic. **Life Expectancy**: 48.09 years. **Human Development Index Rank**: 94.

Scripture

Yet, O LORD, you are our Father; we are the clay, and you are our potter; we are all the work of your hand (Isa. 64:8).

REPUBLIC OF SOUTH AFRICA

A Partnership to Fight HIV/AIDS

With over 4.2 million people infected with HIV/AIDS, South Africa has the largest number of people living with the disease in the world. Mission co-worker Cindy Easterday works with African Enterprise HIV/AIDS ministry and writes about the plight of South Africans. "The devastation this is causing in the lives of our people is staggering. We are losing our educated, our professionals, our vibrant men and women of hope and promise, leaving younger children and older people to carry on as their parents and children die."

The African Enterprise ministry has the mission to evangelize through word and deed, in partnership with the

An association of HIV/AIDS patients meets to provide mutual support.

church. African Enterprise's strategy includes efforts to draw Christian churches of various denominations together and to train and develop Christian leaders. This training enables them to be effective in addressing the problem of HIV/AIDS and to link and support church responses in their communities.

In South Africa this linking strategy poses a unique challenge as racial groups still generally live in separate communities after apartheid. The hope is to link churches, particularly those least impacted and with greater resources to those most greatly impacted and with minimal resources. "Through this strategy we will trust in God for amazing results as Christians begin to 'cross over,' sharing their hearts, talents, and resources and the active love of Jesus Christ with those suffering and in need. Indeed, the earth is the Lord's and all those who live in it. Even in the very worst of circumstances, God is with us," writes Cindy Easterday.

Scripture

Jesus said to them, "Give to the emperor the things that are the emperor's, and to God the things that are God's." And they were utterly amazed at him (Mark 12:17).

Let Us Join in Prayer for:

PC(USA) People in Mission
Joining Hands Against Hunger Network: **Rev. Dr. Kay-Robert Volkwijn**, companionship facilitator, **Desiré Eileen Volkwijn**, team ministry; **Cynthia E. Easterday**, coordinator, AIDS Ministry Program, African Enterprise; **Janet Ellen Guyer**, Southern Africa AIDS regional consultant, Evangelical Presbyterian Church in South Africa; **Barbara Carroll Snyder**, evangelism/new church development, Presbyterian Church (U.S.A.); **Rev. Robert Paul Snyder**, evangelism/new church development, Presbyterian Church (U.S.A.); **Dr. Douglas James Tilton**, parliamentary advocacy, South Africa Council of Churches (SACC)

Partners/Ministries
Evangelical Presbyterian Church in South Africa: **Rev. Ng Tswane**, president; Presbyterian Church of Africa: **Dr. Jabulani E. Mdlalose**, general secretary; Uniting Presbyterian Church in Southern Africa: **Rev. Dr. Max Chigwida**, moderator, **Rev. Alastair Rodger**, general secretary; Uniting Reformed Church in Southern Africa: **Rev. Leonardo A. Appies**, synod secretary

PC(USA) General Assembly Staff
Nikki Bryant, BOP
Elder Andrew Buckley, CMD

Daily Lectionary

Ps. 27, 36, 80, 147:12-20
Isa. 65:1-12
1 Tim. 4:1-16; Mark 12:13-27

Let Us Join in Prayer for:

PC(USA) People in Mission
Presbyterian Church of Mozambique
(IPM): **Rev. Charles William
Wonnenberg**, team ministry,
Rev. Diane Carlson Wonnenberg,
evangelism facilitator

Partners/Ministries
IPM: **Rev. Mario Nyamuxwe**, president
of the Synod Council; Christian Council
in Mozambique: **Bishop João Somane
Machado**, president; Refugee Repatriation
and Resettlement; Ricatla Seminary
Development Office

PC(USA) General Assembly Staff
Ervin Bullock, CMD
Cherrie Burch, FDN
Pamela Burdine, WMD

MOZAMBIQUE

Until a ceasefire was agreed upon in 1992, Mozambique had seen nearly seventeen years of brutal civil war. Ranked as one of the poorest countries in the world, Mozambique has faced daunting challenges as it continues to rebuild. A mission co-worker, the Rev. Diane Wonnenberg, writes about her family's preparation for ministry in Mozambique. "In Chicago, during the 2000 missionary orientation, lying on the narrow dorm bed in the July heat, late at night, I cried out for a word from the Lord. I read Psalm 65. I read it through once and was very unimpressed. I read it a second and then a third time, wondering what could be the significance of this very matter-of-fact agricultural psalm. It is a word picture of a happy people celebrating their God and the blessings of the land. From the few sources available I knew that Mozambique was an agricultural country harrowed by decades of wars, drought, floods, and world-ranking poverty. What did Psalm 65 have to do with Mozambique? Reading it one more time out loud I felt a welling up in my heart. It was as if I was being challenged by this psalm of blessing to ask, 'Can you believe this for Mozambique?'"

Charles and Diane Wonnenberg, evangelism facilitators for the Igreja Presbiteriana de Moçambique (IPM), the PC(USA) partner in Mozambique, work to help fulfill the vision of the IPM to bring healing and growth to the country. Two specific mission emphases of the IPM are outreach with refugees and tribal peoples and the promotion of agricultural projects to stimulate economic development and better stewardship of the land.

photo by Diane Wonnenberg

*Maria Mandlate, wife of the pastor
of the congregation in
Chimoio, Mozambique, is proud
of a beautiful onion harvest.*

Total Area: 302,400 sq. mi. (slightly less than twice the size of California). **Population**: 19,371,057.
Languages: Portuguese (official), indigenous dialects. **GDP Per Capita**: $1,000. **Literacy**: 42.3%
(Male 58.4%, Female 27%). **Religions**: indigenous beliefs, Christian, Muslim. **Life Expectancy**: 36.45
years. **Human Development Index Rank**: 157.

Daily Lectionary
Ps. 32, 130, 139, 148; Isa. 65:17-25
1 Tim. 5:(1-16) 17-22 (23-25)
Mark 12:28-34

Scripture
Before they call I will answer, while they are yet speaking I will hear (Isa. 65:24).

ZAMBIA

Bob and Bobbi Snyder, mission co-workers, work with PC(USA)'s partners in southern Africa—specifically those in Zimbabwe, Mozambique, Malawi, Zambia, and Madagascar. Their work has a dual focus on building churches and schools and nurturing leadership development. They share with us the worship experience at the Matero congregation in west Lusaka, Zambia, on the first Sunday following the September 11 attacks in the United States. "The service was truly exhilarating. The youth choir sang during the service and continued when the service was over. Prayers for the United States were offered three times during the three-hour service. An offering was taken for the victims of the attacks. It included several bills, a few coins, and an egg. This offering, taken for victims in the United States, was given by victims of the violence of poverty. We will long remember the Matero congregation and the worship we shared with them."

Total Area: 285,700 sq. mi. (slightly larger than Texas). **Population**: 9,770,199. **Languages**: English (official), 7 major vernaculars and about 70 other indigenous languages. **GDP Per Capita**: $880. **Literacy**: 78.2% (Male 85.6%, Female 71.3%). **Religions**: Christian, Muslim, Hindu, indigenous beliefs. **Life Expectancy**: 37.29 years. **Human Development Index Rank**: 143.

ZIMBABWE

Like salt, the work and witness of the Uniting Presbyterian Church in Southern Africa (UPCSA) the Presbytery of Zimbabwe have given glory to God," writes Max T. Chigwida, moderator of the General Assembly of the UPCSA. "The UPCSA is one of the oldest churches in the country. It is neither one of the big denominations nor one of the small ones. Nevertheless, like salt, its work and witness have given glory to God." The church's ministry is spread in both rural and urban areas. Its membership is very diverse racially, tribally, nationally, and culturally.

The Presbytery of Zimbabwe asks for prayer for its work in such key ministry areas as children at risk, educational programs for all age levels, HIV/AIDS awareness and home-based care, pastoral care to students at the church's schools, ecumenical collaboration, leadership/ministerial training, evangelism and outreach, and church extension/planting.

Total Area: 149,100 sq. mi. (slightly larger than Montana). **Population**: 11,365,366. **Languages**: English (official), Shona, Sindebele, tribal dialects. **GDP Per Capita**: $2,500. **Religions**: syncretic (part Christian, part indigenous beliefs), Christian, indigenous beliefs, Muslim, other. **Literacy**: 85% (Male 90%, Female 80%). **Life Expectancy**: 37.13 years. **Human Development Index Rank**: 117.

Scripture

Fight the good fight of the faith; take hold of the eternal life, to which you were called and for which you made the good confession in the presence of many witnesses (1 Tim. 6:12).

Let Us Join in Prayer for:

PC(USA) People in Mission
Rev. Leisa TonieAnn Wagstaff, training coordinator/office manager, Association of Christian Lay Centers in Africa [Zimbabwe]

Partners/Ministries
United Church of Zambia (UCZ): **Rev. Harris S. Silishebo**, general secretary; Christian Council of Zambia; Christian Hospital Association of Zambia (CHAZ): **Ms. G. Haimbé**, director; Church of Central Africa Presbyterian (CCAP) Synod of Zambia: **Rev. Victor Chilenje**, general secretary, **Rev. David Chiboboka**, assistant general secretary; Mindolo Ecumenical Foundation [Zambia]; The Uniting Presbyterian Church in Southern Africa (UPCSA), Synod of Zambia: **Rev. Aman Kasambala Kabwata**, moderator; Mbreshi and Mwandi hospitals [Zambia]; Church of Central Africa Presbyterian (CCAP) Synod of Harare [Zimbabwe]: **Joseph Juma**, general secretary; The Uniting Presbyterian Church in Southern Africa (UPCSA), Presbytery of Zimbabwe: **Rev. Wilbert R. Sayimani**, presbytery clerk; Zimbabwe Christian Council: **Rev. Densen Mafinyani**, general secretary, **Rt. Rev. Jonathan Siyachitema**, president; Presbytery Partnership with the UPCSA [Zimbabwe]: Presbytery of Philadelphia

PC(USA) General Assembly Staff
Ruth Burks, CMD
Janie Burton, CMD

Daily Lectionary

Ps. 56, 111, 118, 149
Isa. 66:1-6
1 Tim. 6:(1-5) 6-21; Mark 12:35-44

Camp and Conference Ministries Emphasis

THE LORD'S DAY

MINUTE FOR MISSION
CAMP AND CONFERENCE MINISTRIES

**Sunday Lectionary
and Hymns**

Isa. 43:18–25
The Desert Shall Rejoice
PH 18

Ps. 41
The Church of Christ in Every Age
PH 421

2 Cor. 1:18–22
Amen, Amen
PH 299

Mark 2:1–12
Have Mercy, Lord, on Me
PH 395

Ever so slowly, imperceptibly stretching for the sun, the minute maple seedling pushed aside the dark humus. Its new life was almost stomped out by the hard sole of Anthony's shoe. It wasn't done maliciously—Anthony didn't even think to look. The brick and concrete of his normal city world excluded seedlings. Shaundra, our camp's environmental education counselor, fascinated Anthony and our cabin group, recalling the cycle of the forest from seedling to sapling to mature tree to new seeds—and how precious to God was each new bud in the forest, each newly hatched egg, each newborn babe.

Children gather at Presbyterian camps to share the word of God and worship in the great out-of-doors.

In today's Old Testament Scripture, Isa. 43:18–25, the Lord asks whether we perceive the new thing God is doing here and now. Our lives are not set in concrete. The buds of new life God gives us through the saving grace of Jesus Christ are not burdened with our past sins.

Each year thousands of children, youth, and adults gather at one of our Presbyterian camps or conference centers to refresh their souls and commit or recommit their lives to Jesus Christ, the source of new life. What better place to renew and restore one's spirit than a camp or conference center? Please pray for the faithful, loving Christian leaders and campers as they share the word of God through Bible studies, prayer, breaking bread together, and worship in God's great out-of-doors.

—Rev. Edward Craxton, associate director, Christian Education

Daily Lectionary
Ps. 46, 67, 93, 150
Isa. 66:7-14
1 John 3:4-10; John 10:7-16

Prayer
Thank you for the new life we can know through our Lord, Jesus Christ. Refresh us with new understandings and a new appreciation of each day's possibilities for service and love. Through Jesus Christ we pray. Amen.

ANGOLA

April 2002 brought a ceasefire to the war that has ravaged this country for more than two decades. The fighting has driven almost a third of its thirteen million people from their homes and inflicted disease on a scale seen in few other places in the world. As a result, a resource-rich country with gold, diamonds, extensive forests, Atlantic fisheries, and large oil deposits now ranks as one of the world's poorest nations.

Church World Service (CWS), with contributions from One Great Hour of Sharing, is raising funds for food, household items, blankets, seeds, and tools, as

Villagers from Caxito relax after an evangelistic meeting.

well as for health centers and education projects. CWS is also providing assistance to about 40,000 displaced war survivors living in deplorable conditions in the central areas of the country.

The churches of Angola have also had struggles and hardships during these difficult times. "The church has faced a great deal of persecution, but God gave the victory," writes the Rev. Antonio Mussaqui, the General Secretary for Communication and Literature of the General Synod of the Presbyterian Church of Angola.

"For a long time in the life of Angola, the government policy was against God and the church. In schools children were taught that God does not exist. The first President of Angola, Dr. A. A. Neto, was heard to say in 1976 that twenty years should be enough time to destroy the church and bury it forever. This did not happen. After he died in 1979 the church started growing rapidly and became much stronger. The Christian church has been working to spread the good news of salvation and trying to bring about the healing of the nation."

Total Area: 480,800 sq. mi. (slightly less than twice the size of Texas). **Population**: 10,366,031. **Languages**: Portuguese (official), Bantu, other African languages. **GDP Per Capita**: $1,000. **Literacy**: 42% (Male 56%, Female 28%). **Religions**: indigenous beliefs, Roman Catholic, Protestant. **Life Expectancy**: 38.59 years. **Human Development Index Rank**: 146.

Scripture

Sing praises to God, sing praises; sing praises to our King, sing praises (Ps. 47:6).

Let Us Join in Prayer for:

Partners/Ministries
Presbyterian Church of Angola (IPA):
Rev. Pedro Mateus, president of the general synod

PC(USA) General Assembly Staff
Jennifer Butler, CMD
William Bynum, OGA
Kelly Cahill, BOP

Daily Lectionary

Ps. 47, 57, 85, 145
Ruth 1:1-14
2 Cor. 1:1-11; Matt. 5:1-12

Let Us Join in Prayer for:

Synod Staff
Rev. J. Grant Lowe,
interim synod executive
Mary Taaffe, administrative assistant
Elder Diana J. Barber, associate executive,
leadership development
Donn McLellan, associate executive,
communication and interpretation
Elder Ernest E. Cutting, stated clerk
Elder Patricia Milloy,
administrative assistant
Elder Billie Novy, associate,
administration and operations
Jackie Palmer, accounting assistant,
payroll and administrative assistant
Elder Laurie Reis, financial assistant
Lori Sheehy, desktop/applications
administrator and webmaster
Rev. Kathryn Smith, synod
school administrator
Elder Elona Street-Stewart, program
staff, racial ethnic ministries and
community empowerment
Elder Sandra K. Wagener, associate
executive, mission and stewardship
Elder J. Jay Wilkinson, director of finance
and treasurer

PC(USA) General Assembly Staff
Claire Calhoun, PW
Carolina Callender-Mora, NMD
Barbara Campbell, DEDO

Daily Lectionary

Ps. 28, 54, 99, 146
Ruth 1:15-22
2 Cor. 1:12-22; Matt. 5:13-20

THE SYNOD OF LAKES AND PRAIRIES

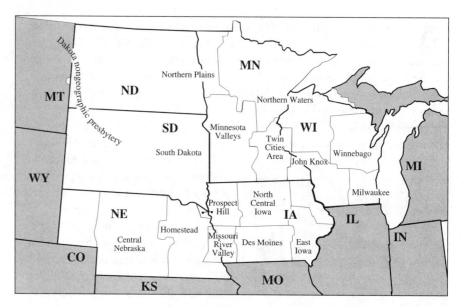

In 2000 the Synod of Lakes and Prairies created a Committee on Congregational Development. It is charged with developing and overseeing a synod-wide strategy for church development and redevelopment, working in concert with the presbyteries. It includes ministry to and with existing racial ethnic communities and congregations as well as new immigrant populations.

Favorable economic opportunities in the Midwest are a draw to many immigrants. People from Southeast Asia and Africa (especially Sudan), as well as Spanish-speaking countries, have moved within the synod's bounds, providing all presbyteries with outreach opportunities. With support from the presbyteries of Des Moines and Missouri River Valley and the General Assembly, the synod hired a coordinator of Sudanese ministry in 2002 to provide resourcing and support for Sudanese fellowships, host congregations, and presbyteries with Sudanese immigrants.

The Synod of Lakes and Prairies has 946 churches and 178,902 members. The University of Dubuque Theological Seminary is located within the synod's bounds.

Scripture

Ruth said, "Do not press me to leave you or to turn back from following you! Where you go, I will go; where you lodge, I will lodge; your people shall be my people, and your God my God" (Ruth 1:16).

THE PRESBYTERY OF CENTRAL NEBRASKA

The Presbytery of Central Nebraska, where close to one-third of the congregations minister without pastoral leadership, has turned to its own resources in moving the church ahead in its mission to rural America. The vast Nebraska prairie is rich in resources for nurturing the land. It is also rich in dedicated lay people who know what it is like to be the church in the heartland.

The Commissioned Lay Pastor Training Program is meeting the church's needs at home by training and mentoring elders for service. This two-year program, run in conjunction with the Lay Pastor Institute at Sterling College in Sterling, Kansas, has prepared ten men and women for service as commissioned lay pastors (CLPs) in the last ten years. Currently, six of those individuals are commissioned to local congregations.

Where it may not be feasible for small churches to attract ministers of Word and Sacrament (all six of the CLP-pastored churches have fewer than 130 members), these congregations have turned to resources in their own backyards. All of the six CLPs currently serving are Nebraska natives who were living and working in the areas that surround their congregations before receiving their training. Perhaps more so than ordained clergy moving in from other parts of the country, CLPs here have keen insight into the issues and problems facing their parishioners. They are able to relate well and thereby minister effectively.

The Committee on Preparation for Ministry and the Committee on Ministry now view the Commissioned Lay Pastor Training Program as an important piece of the presbytery's plan to secure quality leadership for its churches. Tapping into resources at home has become an effective way to meet the many needs of a faithful people.

The Presbytery of Central Nebraska has 7,185 members in 42 churches.

Let Us Join in Prayer for:

Elder Bruce C. Hendrickson,
member, GAC

Presbytery Staff
Rev. Robert E. Houser,
executive presbyter
Rev. James Hawley, stated clerk
Angela Palmer, administrative assistant

PC(USA) General Assembly Staff
Carolyn Campbell, MSS
Rev. Dr. Donald G. Campbell, CMD
Deanna Carcelli, WMD

Scripture

For we are the aroma of Christ to God among those who are being saved . . . a fragrance from life to life (2 Cor. 2:15–16).

Daily Lectionary

Ps. 65, 91, 125, 147:1-11
Ruth 2:1-13
2 Cor. 1:23–2:17; Matt. 5:21-26

THE PRESBYTERY OF DAKOTA

Nongeographic

Let Us Join in Prayer for:

Presbytery Staff
Rev. Michael Simon, stated clerk, acting administrative officier
Elder Joan Broomfield, treasurer

PC(USA) General Assembly Staff
Bernellyn Carey, BOP
Nohra Carrillo, CMD
Sylvia Carter, MSS

The wind blows pretty hard across the plains, and few have any better stories about rainstorms, snowy blizzards, floods, and tornadoes than the elders in the communities served by the churches in the Presbytery of Dakota.

Located across the upper plains and the river valleys of Minnesota, North and South Dakota, and eastern Montana, the twenty-one churches in the presbytery rest on hill bluffs or prairie flats and truly provide a welcome despite the tough environment and shortage of pastors. It is not unusual to look out the window during the worship service to see cows wandering just outside or tumbleweeds. Here, members and visitors alike reckon with the forces of nature and social disparity in ways that evoke the most humble expressions of faith and the richness of family relationships.

Bdecan Church's new sanctuary was completed by volunteers from Northern Plains Presbytery.

Last year, the Pejuhutazizi Church in Granite Falls, Minnesota, experienced its second one-hundred-year flood within five years. Recalling the previous disaster, experienced members quickly emptied the building of all furnishings at the first warning, but the flood circled under the sanctuary rather than through it and the foundation was crushed. Cooperative solutions with tribal government and volunteer labor jacked up the building and moved it to higher ground. Presbyterian Disaster Assistance provided funding for the new foundation and necessary hookups.

Farther north, flooding created polluted groundwater in the Devils Lake area of North Dakota. Again Presbyterian Disaster Assistance funded new well and sewer provisions, and volunteer labor from churches in the Presbytery of the Northern Plains completed a new sanctuary for the Bdecan Church in Tokio. Joyful dedication services occurred in the spring of 2002.

The Dakota Presbytery has 914 members in 21 congregations.

Daily Lectionary

Ps. 81, 116, 143, 147:12-20
Ruth 2:14-23; 2 Cor. 3:1-18
Matt. 5:27-37

Scripture
"Let your word be 'Yes, Yes' or 'No, No'; anything more than this comes from the evil one" (Matt. 5:37).

THE PRESBYTERY OF DES MOINES

Iowa

Is Genesis just a collection of myths, or does it contain lessons to be learned by people today? The Sunday school class at First Presbyterian Church, Malcom, Iowa, has examined Genesis as a foundation of a Christian's beliefs.

The class drew a timeline on a long piece of fabric and hung it on the wall of the fellowship room. The first lesson sketched onto the timeline was about the Trinity and how God is the Alpha and Omega. Next, the life of Jesus and the cross were drawn in, taking the class from the year before his death to the year after his death.

Kristina and Bryan Helleso, Molly Bailey, and teacher Alice Waechter studied the book of Genesis.

The class's attention went back to the creation accounts. One important question asked by a student was "How could God make light on the first day if the sun wasn't made until the fourth day?" This was a good time to learn about God's omnipotence, the mystery of faith, and the Bible's purpose in presenting the summary of God's creation in this order.

God's providence became the next focus. The mighty power of God, who holds creation in the palm of God's hand, was demonstrated with a glove. The glove soon held the end of a thread that was sewn through the entire timeline, demonstrating God's plan for saving humanity, that is, the redemption God offers by the sacrifice and resurrection of Christ.

The students and many adult members of the church have drawn in their names, dates of birth, and lifelines up to the present as a way of reflecting that all are a part of God's creation.

The Presbytery of Des Moines includes 65 churches with 11,564 members.

Scripture

O LORD, God of my salvation, when, at night, I cry out in your presence, let my prayer come before you; incline your ear to my cry (Ps. 88:1–2).

Let Us Join in Prayer for:

Elder Pamila G. Deichmann, member, GAC

Presbytery Staff
Rev. Philip W. Barrett, general presbyter, stated clerk
Joyce Cole, office manager
Mary Ann Van Liew, administrative assistant
Elder Nancy Lister-Settle, hunger action enabler

PC(USA) General Assembly Staff
April Case, DEDO
Debbie Cassady, PILP
Sharon Castillo, BOP

Daily Lectionary

Ps. 6, 20, 88, 148
Ruth 3:1-18; 2 Cor. 4:1-12
Matt. 5:38-48

Let Us Join in Prayer for:

Elder Mary Jane Jakobsen,
member, GAC

Presbytery Staff
Elder Harry D. Olthoff, general
presbyter/facilatator
Rev. R. Dixon Jennings, stated clerk
Rev. Paul R. Skelley, treasurer
Pamela Prather, administrative
assistant/finance
Laura Gadola, administrative
assistant/communications
Joy E. Bayshore, administrative
assistant/meetings and schedules

PC(USA) General Assembly Staff
Rhonda Cates, BOP
Janice Catron, PPC
Kelley Caudill, DEDO

THE PRESBYTERY OF EAST IOWA

A number of congregations in the Presbytery of East Iowa are exploring new ways of reaching out to meet the needs of people in their communities. After-school programs with an emphasis on working with special children, parenting programs, and family-night-out programs are examples of an emerging emphasis on children and family ministries. Others, particularly in smaller communities, are developing ecumenical youth programs. Many are experimenting with different ways of communicating during worship that allow younger generations greater access to the worship of God and older generations joy in seeing faith bloom among new people in their midst. Emphasis also is being placed on events and training that focus on reaching people through community service and worship.

The desire to deepen awareness of connectedness with all other people is being demonstrated in congregations through a wide range of programs. One small congregation is helping children learn about and share with other people through their weekly Sunday school offering. Each class is selecting the people and ministry it wishes to support. Several congregations are actively engaged in learning about Islam in the wake of September 11, 2001.

The presbytery as a whole is deepening its awareness in two special ways. A renewed interest in staying abreast of the Israeli-Palestinian dilemma is keeping the Rev. Darrell Yeaney, retired campus minister and Middle East peacemaking enabler, busy resourcing and teaching people. The Rev. Mike Spangler, the presbytery enabler for the international partnership with the Presbytery of Ceara in northeastern Brazil, coordinated a trip to Ceara in July 2002 for a multigenerational group from eight congregations.

Elder Harry Olthoff has been welcomed and installed as the general presbyter. He will lead the presbytery into a new vision with renewed energy as a community of congregations participating in God's mission for these days. He begins with a people who believe that the earth and all who dwell therein belong to God.

The Presbytery of East Iowa has 17,735 members in 84 churches.

Daily Lectionary

Ps. 63, 100, 122, 149
Ruth 4:1-22
2 Cor. 4:13–5:10; Matt. 6:1-6

Scripture
For we know that if the earthly tent we live in is destroyed, we have a building from God, a house not made with hands, eternal in the heavens (2 Cor. 5:1).

THE LORD'S DAY

MINUTE FOR MISSION
COLUMBIA THEOLOGICAL SEMINARY

In the midst of urban sprawl, commercial development, and general busyness, many of us find ourselves in need of a place to get away to—to walk in the woods, to pray in a garden, or to join together in growing fruits and vegetables. Members of the Columbia Seminary community and neighborhood are able daily to enjoy such a place.

The woods surrounding the seminary's athletic field and garden are a part of the local community's commitment to preserve green space throughout the city. In addition, Columbia's campus is home to one of ten gardens around the world that are set apart by the nonprofit, nondenominational organization Gardens for Peace—places for meditation and peace in the midst of a world at war.

Another place where members of the greater community gather as Christ's body is in the community garden. Columbia students and families, staff, and international students, in addition to seventh graders from a community school, gather together to nurture this green pocket of organic land. A grape arbor, a labyrinth, and an herb garden overlook the rows of collectively grown strawberries, blueberries, and raspberries.

In the midst of exams and papers, presentations and internships, students and friends can locate those spaces to find peace in the midst of God's good creation as they are nurtured for their service to Jesus Christ and Christ's church.

photo by: Laura Bordeaux

Columbia Seminary students and families enjoy the community garden.

—*Katie Ricks, student, Columbia Theological Seminary*

Prayer
Creator God, we ask that you continue to provide us with spaces for Sabbath time and people with whom we can rest in your presence. We give you thanks for all of your creation that provides places for discernment, peace, and community. In Christ's name. Amen.

Sunday Lectionary and Hymns

2 Kings 2:1–12
I Sing the Mighty Power of God
PH 288; HB 84

Ps. 50:1–6
God of Compassion, in Mercy Befriend Us
PH 261; HB 122; PPCS 45

2 Cor. 4:3–6
Christ, Whose Glory Fills the Skies
PH 462; HB 47

Mark 9:2–9
Swiftly Pass the Clouds of Glory
PH 73

Daily Lectionary

Ps. 103, 117, 139, 150
Dan. 7:9-10, 13-14
2 Cor. 3:1-9; John 12:27-36a

Let Us Join in Prayer for:

Elder Reginald S. Kuhn, member, GAC

Presbytery Staff
Carole Philippi, administrative assistant

PC(USA) General Assembly Staff
Nancy Cavalcante, NMD
Elder Donald Cecil, DEDO
Rev. David H. Chai, CMD

HOMESTEAD PRESBYTERY
Nebraska

The gently rolling hills of northeastern Nebraska are cherished and farmed by hearty folks, some of whom are Presbyterians of the rural Unity Parish (First Presbyterian in Wakefield and John Hus Presbyterian in Thurston). The strong Czech heritage of many citizens of this region is a testament to their respect for and care of the land and also of their great faith commitment and regard for the ancestors who immigrated there many years ago to farm and plant churches.

Mission volunteer Jane Kilgore joins presbytery mission coordinator Arta Smith and a member of the parish council beside John Hus Church.

During conversations between the parish council and the Rev. Sue Banholzer about ways to revitalize its witness in the region, this small parish asked the presbytery to assist in developing some new visions for the new millennium. Meanwhile, Elder Jane Kilgore of Peace River Presbytery in Florida was hoping to be a short-term mission volunteer in another part of the country and submitted her application to Homestead Presbytery's Mission Volunteers with Small Churches program.

Jane's outstanding qualifications seemed an excellent match for Unity Parish, and she subsequently spent three weeks sharing her own unique gifts and vitality with these Nebraskan Presbyterians. Jane helped the parish council renew its lost tradition of a monthly parish newsletter, assisted the John Hus congregation with starting an adult Sunday school, and brought supplemental children's educational materials to the teachers of the Wakefield congregation. Jane's refreshing presence was a reminder to the congregations that "the earth is the LORD's and all . . . those who live in it."

Homestead Presbytery has 63 congregations and 11,572 members.

Daily Lectionary

Ps. 5, 29, 82, 145
Deut. 6:1-15
Heb. 1:1-14; John 1:1-18

Scripture
Lead me, O LORD, in your righteousness because of my enemies; make your way straight before me (Ps. 5:8).

THE PRESBYTERY OF THE JOHN KNOX
Iowa, Minnesota, Wisconsin

People in Tel Aviv have heard of it, but in Dallas they may have no idea where Postville, Iowa, is. This upper midwestern town in the Presbytery of the John Knox has seen an influx of immigrants from Israel and Mexico, among other places. The area has become a microcosm of the world, thanks in great part to the kosher slaughterhouse that replaced a meat processing plant and to the community of Lubavitcher Jews associated with the plant.

Initially, many of the new citizens of Postville faced bigotry and anti-Semitic attitudes and actions. These struggles are outlined in the book *Postville: A Clash of Cultures in Heartland America*, written by Stephen Bloom. In response, the leaders of the community and churches of Postville invited citizens to come together and to sign a resolution against such actions.

Though the community continues to struggle with the issues faced by a changing population, a friendliness has begun to surface. Throughout the community people have been breaking down the barriers of religion, nationality, and race. Community Presbyterian Church of Postville has joined other churches and organizations to find ways in which people of all nations and religions can live together. Community Presbyterian Church participates in this multicultural experience by sharing its sanctuary on Saturdays for an evangelical Guatemalan worship service; providing space in the church's kitchen for Filipinos and Ukrainians to prepare food for the Taste of Postville held each August; being treated on Consecration Sunday to a kosher meal; and singing the closing hymn in English and Spanish at the annual ecumenical Thanksgiving service.

It is the prayer of Community Presbyterian Church that these efforts can be an example for others in Postville and around the world to live together in peace across cultural, religious, and racial lines.

The Presbytery of the John Knox has 11,407 members in 64 churches.

Let Us Join in Prayer for:

Presbytery Staff
Rev. Hal Murry, executive presbyter
Rev. Ken Meunier,
associate executive presbyter
Elder Alyson Janke, stated clerk
Rosemary Buchholz, secretary
Judy Crotsensberg,
presbytery administrator

PC(USA) General Assembly Staff
David Chao, PPC
Rev. Jon Chapman, WMD

Scripture
You shall say to your children, "We were Pharaoh's slaves in Egypt, but the LORD brought us out of Egypt with a mighty hand" (Deut. 6:21).

Daily Lectionary
Ps. 42, 102, 133, 146
Deut. 6:16-25
Heb. 2:1-10; John 1:19-28

Let Us Join in Prayer for:

PC(USA) General Assembly Staff
Elder Patricia Chapman, NMD
Sandra Charles, EDO
Kathleen Chase, BOP

ASH WEDNESDAY

MINUTE FOR MISSION

Why are people coming to the church?" I asked several Christian church leaders in different parts of China not too long ago. Churches there are not permitted to advertise, hold revival meetings, or call attention to themselves or their faith in public places; yet they have been growing rapidly, mainly because of the previously unchurched.

Leaders responded that each individual Christian participates in evangelism by example. Sermons and homilies are aimed at teaching members how to live a Christian life, to treat neighbors and friends with the love of Christ. The result is that the Christian community shines brightly and becomes attractive to others. "Every day we have newcomers," testified one church leader.

What are the Chinese church members doing that is so attractive?

They visit congregation members in the hospital, not just one person or one visit, but many persons and many visits. Other patients and their families remark, "See how Christians care for each other!" They actively participate in society, in work to improve people's lives. The word gets out, "Christians work for the good of the public—of all—not just for themselves!" They are peacemakers. When household quarrels continue to erupt and seem intractable, neighbors suggest, "Maybe you should go to the Christian church; those people don't quarrel!"

Chinese Christians honor the work of Presbyterian missionaries and others who laid the foundation for the work of their church today. They are eager to share the good news.

Isaiah speaks of the true worship of God, that which brings honor to God: not outward signs of "being religious," but the God-blessed signs of sharing with and caring for those who cannot care for themselves and for living in mutual respect and harmony (Isa. 58:1-12). "Then your light shall rise in the darkness . . . you shall be like a watered garden, like a spring of water, whose waters never fail."

On Ash Wednesday, as we enter a time of study and reflection when we mourn for our sins and prepare for renewal, let us continue to work to be examples of a Christian community that shines brightly.

—Rev. Dr. Barbara A. Renton, chair, General Assembly Council

Daily Lectionary

Ps. 5, 27, 51, 147:1-11
Jon. 3:1–4:11
Heb. 12:1-14; Luke 18:9-14

Prayer
O God, we thank you for the steadfast witness of Christians past and present. By your Spirit, strengthen our hearts for service, which is the worship you desire. Grant us the presence of your Son, Jesus Christ, to journey with us during this season of Lent and times of testing, that our words and deeds may honor you. In Jesus' name. Amen.

THE PRESBYTERY OF MILWAUKEE

Wisconsin

In response to the 202nd General Assembly's call to sustain and restore God's creation, Grace Presbyterian Church in Beaver Dam, Wisconsin, recognized its responsibility to heal and protect creation and launched a plan to replace a piece of church lawn with prairie grasses and flowers. The project began with designing the garden and meeting with the city council and neighbors. The session allocated $500 for the garden. The work of preparing the soil for planting brought together church members, friends, and a high school environmental class, along with city tree trimmers to complete the project. The Graceful Prairie has become a place to sense the beauty and diversity of God's awesome creation. Black-eyed Susans, coneflowers, asters, goldenrod, daisies, primrose, Indian grass, and wild Canada rye flourish. Unlike a lawn, the garden requires no watering, no fertilizers, no herbicides, and no weekly mowing.

The Graceful Prairie, planted by members of Grace Presbyterian Church in Beaver Dam, is a place of beauty.

In another corner of the presbytery, West Granville Presbyterian sought to beautify some of its church grounds. The Christian education committee suggested a butterfly garden that could be developed as a place of prayer and outdoor worship. During the following year the plans were developed. Then congregation members moved dirt and stone, created a drainage system, added a walking path, and installed benches. Afterward church members gathered under sunny skies to plant more than eight hundred perennials. The West Granville Prayer Garden now offers a quiet place for contemplation and prayer.

The Presbytery of Milwaukee in southeastern Wisconsin is home to rich diversity among its 11,884 Presbyterians in 50 churches. Carroll College and Presbyterian Homes of Wisconsin also flourish here.

Scripture

[John] saw Jesus coming toward him and declared, "Here is the Lamb of God who takes away the sin of the world!" (John 1:29).

Let Us Join in Prayer for:

Presbytery Staff
Rev. Philip C. Brown, executive presbyter
Rev. Roy Godwin,
interim associate executive
Elder Eileen Pierce, program coordinator
Elder Florence Sampson,
corporate administrator
Elder Roxanne Lawrence,
resource center coordinator
Elder Judy Bell, stated clerk
Elder Detlef Pavlovich, treasurer

PC(USA) General Assembly Staff
Rev. Eric Chavis, FDN
Brian Chmielinski, BOP
Teresa Chrappa, WMD

Daily Lectionary

Ps. 27, 102, 126, 147:12-20
Deut. 7:6-11
Titus 1:1-16; John 1:29-34

Let Us Join in Prayer for:

PC(USA) General Assembly Staff
Bridget Clancy, OGA
Dorothy Clark, BOP
Martha Clark, EDO

WORLD DAY OF PRAYER

MINUTE FOR MISSION

On this World Day of Prayer, we join with Christians around the world in prayer for God's people everywhere. Prayer begins in a grateful awareness of God at work in the world.

The World Day of Prayer began in the nineteenth century as women in the church called for prayers for mission, especially for women and children. Over the years and out of historic experiences of war and need, the call to prayer focused on mission unity and, especially, world peace.

Recently, Worldwide Ministries had a partnership consultation with international partner churches. When asked how we could help, our partners called us first to pray for them. As they talked, it was apparent that this was not out of politeness or theological correctness. They were grateful for our support of their work, but what they really need is God present with and through and around them. The most important help we can give is prayer.

Lebanese church leaders wrote materials for the 2003 World Day of Prayer.

God is good and is indeed at work in the world in matters small and large. God is good and hears our prayers—spoken in any language. Thanks be to God.

—*Rev. William C. Browne, associate director, Ecumenical Partnership*

Prayer

Gracious God, we pray for your people around the world. We pray that you would gift us with peace and deep gladness. Call us as your church to a more energetic and faithful unity as the body of Christ, in whose name we pray. Amen.

THE PRESBYTERY OF MINNESOTA VALLEYS

Thirty-five miles is a long winter's drive to church in north central Minnesota. So in 1991, four couples began meeting for informal worship. The presbytery conducted a feasibility probe.

"Not yet" was the answer to the request for a new church development at Crosslake on the beautiful Whitefish chain of lakes. Week after week the small fellowship met and grew as summer cottages became permanent residences for retirees from Minnesota, Iowa, Kansas, Nebraska, Washington, D.C., and elsewhere.

Crosslake's new building is on the beautiful Whitefish chain of lakes in central Minnesota.

Resourced by a series of retired clergy and a lay pastor, the group steadily grew. The presbytery's purchase of a building site and call of an organizing pastor boosted morale and numbers. Cash gifts and pledges to cover loans and the program budget made construction possible. The selection of ground source heating meant reduced energy costs and a witness of ecological responsibility.

An outdoor amphitheater and hiking trail have been created on the church's 10-acre site. Whitefish Chautauqua, a nonprofit organization, is being created to host cultural, educational, and theological events to attract tourists and seasonal and permanent residents.

Successfully establishing a new church has confirmed the faith and vision of the founding families. The hymn lines "Seek ye first the kingdom of God, and God's righteousness, and all these things shall be added unto you" are frequently sung with great feeling and conviction, and this was so especially at the chartering of the church by the Presbytery of Minnesota Valleys in May 2002.

The Crosslake Presbyterian new church development and several redevelopments in other towns contribute to a sense of great thanksgiving in the rural Presbytery of Minnesota Valleys, which has 11,828 members in 68 churches.

Scripture

This Spirit [God] poured out on us richly through Jesus Christ our Savior, so that, having been justified by [God's] grace, we might become heirs according to the hope of eternal life (Titus 3:6–7).

Let Us Join in Prayer for:

Presbytery Staff
Rev. Wayne Purintun, executive presbyter
Donna M. Donner, administrative assistant
Elder Karen Houtman, stated clerk
Virginia Molitor, bookkeeper/secretary

PC(USA) General Assembly Staff
Brenda Clarke, BOP
Rev. Carol Clarke, WMD
Marva Clayton-Miles, NMD

Daily Lectionary

Ps. 31, 43, 143, 149
Deut. 7:17-26
Titus 3:1-15; John 1:43-51

Sunday Lectionary and Hymns

Gen. 9:8–17
Great Is Thy Faithfulness
PH 276

Ps. 25:1–10
Lord, to You My Soul Is Lifted
PH 178; PPCS 23

1 Peter 3:18–22
We Know That Christ Is Raised
PH 495

Mark 1:9–15
Lord, Who Throughout These Forty Days
PH 81

THE LORD'S DAY

MINUTE FOR MISSION
CELEBRATE THE GIFTS OF WOMEN

In the familiar Bible story of God's covenant with Noah after the flood, we often overlook the fact that God's covenant extends to all of creation, to "every living creature of all flesh that is on the earth" (Gen. 9:16). A Brief Statement of Faith acknowledges our human failings in honoring God's covenant: "we rebel against God . . . exploit neighbor and nature, and threaten death to the planet entrusted to our care. We deserve God's condemnation. Yet God acts with justice and mercy to redeem creation. In everlasting love, the God of Abraham and Sarah chose a covenant people to bless all families of the earth." As we celebrate the gifts of women this Sunday, we look to National Network of Presbyterian College Women member Kristy Graf, who exemplifies a model of women's liberation in her efforts to restore right relationship with the earth and its inhabitants.

As a student at Cornell University majoring in the historically male-oriented field of biological and environmental engineering, Kristy studies math and science to solve environmental problems, with a focus on sustainable energy. The recognition that "the earth is the LORD's and all . . . those who live in it" (Ps. 24:1) reaffirms her commitment to improving our efficient use of sustainable resources. Her faith perspective helps her to see that her work is part of a much larger picture of God's involvement with humanity. She approaches this work with a focus on a larger world perspective because of her faith in God.

Frederick Buechner writes that God calls us toward a place where our deep joy and the world's deep hunger meet. This is our Christian vocation. Let us celebrate the effort and the gifts of women like Kristy Graf who live out their Christian vocation in pursuit of healing for the world.

—*Gusti L. Newquist, associate, National Network of Presbyterian College Women*

Daily Lectionary

Ps. 32, 42, 84, 150
Jer. 9:23-24
1 Cor. 1:18-31; Mark 2:18-22

Prayer
Healing One, we celebrate today our Christian vocation to restore right relationship with the earth and its inhabitants. May we accept the challenge with joy and thanksgiving as faithful disciples of Jesus Christ, relying on the guidance of the Holy Spirit in every aspect of our living. In Jesus' name. Amen.

THE PRESBYTERY OF MISSOURI RIVER VALLEY   *Iowa, Nebraska*

The Presbytery of Missouri River Valley, set in rural towns and one urban area, puts hands and feet to its concern for the restoration of the earth and its inhabitants. The Southwest Iowa Latino Center in Red Oak, Iowa, has received a Self-Development of People grant to begin a vegetable garden. The center's initial harvest was successful, and those who labored for it willingly shared the results with their neighbors. The director of the project, Jennifer Homer, is confident that the Diversity Community Garden project will continue to attract others and that the common labor will mean continued caring and sharing in the community.

In the presbytery's one urban area, Omaha, most Presbyterian churches have participated for over twenty years in the annual CROP Hunger Walk. One-fourth of the walk's earnings goes to the Omaha Food Bank, which contributes to over three dozen pantries in Nebraska and western Iowa. The area's many thrift stores help out with recycled clothing.

The presbytery has a large Sudanese community. Three Presbyterian churches in Omaha—Central, First, and Mt. View—have worshiping communities of Sudanese. Food, warm clothing, Bibles, English classes, and transportation are among the offerings these new friends have been given by the presbytery.

Gardeners work in the Diversity Community Garden in Red Oak.

Missouri River Valley's Presbyterian Women have been sewing mosquito nets for the Networkers Project to end malaria. They have collected clothing and health kits for mission projects. The presbytery's international partners in Nicaragua received sewing machines through a churchwide effort, and a sewing school has been established. Presbytery members plan to see that their Nicaraguan partners have fabric in order to establish a business there.

The 58 churches with 13,198 members that make up the Presbytery of Missouri River Valley pray for all of these projects and feel closely connected through a common love for Christ.

Scripture
The LORD will keep your going out and your coming in from this time on and forevermore (Ps. 121:8).

Let Us Join in Prayer for:

Presbytery Staff
Rev. Bart Brenner, executive presbyter
Ann Carpenter, resource coordinator
Dr. Russell Palmer, stated clerk
Joan Royer, administrative assistant

PC(USA) General Assembly Staff
Rev. Kerry Clements, OGA
Anita Clemons, FDN
Rev. Dennis Cobb, OGA

Daily Lectionary
Ps. 6, 119:73-80, 121, 145
Deut. 8:1-20
Heb. 2:11-18; John 2:1-12

Let Us Join in Prayer for:

Presbytery Staff
Rev. Neil Brown, executive presbyter
Rev. Ethel Kay Livingston, associate
executive presbyter
Rev. Charles E. Orr, stated clerk
Lloyd Hummel, treasurer
Kaylene Hoskins, administrative assistant
Marty McCrea, resource
center coordinator
John Butler, CONTACT, general editor
William Kay, CONTACT,
layout/design editor
Lynette Hartman, secretary

PC(USA) General Assembly Staff
Amye Cole, CMD
Thyriss Coleman, MSS

THE PRESBYTERY OF NORTH CENTRAL IOWA

As residents of the heartland, also known as the breadbasket that provides food for the world, the 10,224 members of the Presbytery of North Central Iowa's 55 congregations take seriously their responsibility to be good stewards of the land and water that God has committed into their care.

Water quality is a significant problem facing the state of Iowa. Since October 2000, the First Presbyterian Church of Mason City has commissioned an intergenerational team to serve on its Water Monitoring Team. Team members meet once a month to monitor a site on Willow Creek, a stream that runs through Mason City before it joins other streams that eventually flow into the Mississippi. The team monitors the site for stream width and velocity, turbidity, temperature, pH, nitrate, phosphate, chloride, E. coli bacteria, and general coliform bacteria. In addition, three times a year team members gather samplings of benthic macroinvertebrates (bottom-dwelling insects) that inhabit the stream. The presence or absence of

Michael Lalor (front) and Sam Hamilton-Poore collect a monthly water sample.

certain insects may indicate the relative health of the stream. The Water Monitoring Team reports its findings by means of the Internet to the state's volunteer water quality monitoring program, IOWATER.

Due to the interest and support of the congregation, a second team is being formed to monitor an additional site. Monitoring the health of Willow Creek is one very concrete way that First Presbyterian Church seeks to serve and keep the creation that God has entrusted to us.

Daily Lectionary

Ps. 25, 34, 91, 146
Deut. 9:(1-3) 4-12
Heb. 3:1-11; John 2:13-22

Scripture

When they call to me, I will answer them; I will be with them in trouble, I will rescue them and honor them (Ps. 91:15).

THE PRESBYTERY OF THE NORTHERN PLAINS
Minnesota, Montana, North Dakota

Today, change happens on the prairie at a frightening pace. Decisions made by farm and ranch families can be painful. The drastic step of leaving the land and a way of life passed down through the generations is heart wrenching, almost like leaving part of the soul in the soil. Whatever the decision, there is help available and the Lord is faithful.

Lutheran Rural Response (LRR) is one of the many programs of Lutheran Social Services of North Dakota. LRR works directly with individuals and families to address their needs, explore resources, and, if necessary, aid in making transitions. In a move that spans the boundaries of denominations, the Presbytery of Northern Plains has partnered with LRR to offer healing, help, and hope. As a new partner the presbytery will promote the programs of LRR and provide financial support. Bonnie Turner, state director of LRR, conducted a workshop at a presbytery meeting to explain how LRR helps farmers, ranchers, and rural communities identify the stresses and challenges of rural life.

"Presbyterians have always worked ecumenically, and the rich resources of Lutheran Rural Response offer a new opportunity to reach people in need," said the Rev. Arabella Meadows-Rogers, executive presbyter. As part of this new collaboration, the presbytery will emphasize to congregations the services that are available through LRR. Big decisions loom before many of the presbytery's rural parishioners and friends. Together, the presbytery and LRR can make a difference in the lives of those living the rural crisis in North Dakota. There is strength and there is hope!

The Presbytery of the Northern Plains has 8,283 members in 72 churches.

A Presbyterian-Lutheran partnership is helping rural North Dakota.

Let Us Join in Prayer for:

Presbytery Staff
Rev. Arabella Meadows Rogers, executive presbyter
Elder Michael R. Lochow, stated clerk
Laurie Elhard, administrative assistant and bookkeeper

PC(USA) General Assembly Staff
Tiffany Coleman, MSS
Elder Renee Combs, CMD
Rev. Lynn Connette, WMD

Scripture
For we have become partners of Christ, if only we hold our first confidence firm to the end (Heb. 3:14).

Daily Lectionary
Ps. 5, 27, 51, 147:1-11
Deut. 9:13-21
Heb. 3:12-19; John 2:23–3:15

Let Us Join in Prayer for:

Presbytery Staff
Rev. Sharon Johnson, executive presbyter
Elder Nancy Grittman, stated clerk
Elder Karen Habert, treasurer
Jackie Walen, administrative secretary

PC(USA) General Assembly Staff
Lavenna Constant, WMD
Chris Conver, PPC
Elder Donna Cook, NMD

THE PRESBYTERY OF NORTHERN WATERS *Minnesota, Michigan, Wisconsin*

The lives of Presbyterians in the northland have been influenced by distinct and diverse European cultures, a diversity considered precious and something to be celebrated. Presbyterian churches in the northland were often bridge churches to settlers, bringing people of great diversity together while maintaining ancestral celebrations of heritage.

Another diversity that really challenges this area is its geography. The Presbytery of Northern Waters extends over parts of three states (Michigan, Wisconsin, and Minnesota) and covers more than 55,000 square miles. Sometimes the distance between one Presbyterian church and another can prevent the two from feeling attached. The Presbytery of Northern Waters is managing the distance by concentrating efforts on that which can be accomplished. The presbytery council is encouraging every church by 2005 to seek out an unchurched group of people in its community and to consciously be present with that group in an unconventional way.

The Rev. Andrea Krasznai (right), a Reformed airport chaplain from Budapest, Hungary, stayed with the Rev. Marilee Olson during her visit to the presbytery in 2001 as part of the Mission to the U.S.A. program.

Theological diversity is also a challenge. Respecting every person's opinion and treating each person with dignity honor theological diversity. No one is belittled for his or her beliefs; there is no political maneuvering to gain advantage for one side or another.

Currently the Presbytery of Northern Waters is seeking to develop a sister partnership with a presbytery in Central America. By working with different cultures the presbytery can continue to expand its diversity and to celebrate its unity in Christ.

The Presbytery of Northern Waters includes 8,273 members in 63 congregations.

Daily Lectionary

Ps. 27, 102, 126, 147:12-20
Deut. 9:23–10:5; Heb. 4:1-10
John 3:16-21

Scripture
"For God so loved the world that [God] gave [God's] only Son, so that everyone who believes in [God] may not perish but may have eternal life" (John 3:16).

The Presbytery of Prospect Hill *Iowa, Nebraska*

With a bagpiper leading the way, worshipers from First Presbyterian Church (a PC(USA) congregation) and St. Paul's Lutheran Church (an Evangelical Lutheran Church in America congregation) marched from their separate sanctuaries in Rockwell City, Iowa, to meet in the street, shake hands, and share the peace of Christ with each other. This celebration of cooperative ministry was the result of many months, even years, of prayer and discernment in which the two congregations sought to answer the question, "Are there ways our ministries can be enhanced by our finding ways to share worship and mission together rather than separately?"

A piper leads the way as First Presbyterian and St. Paul's Lutheran churches join together.

The answer they discovered was a resounding "yes." On December 2, 2001, the Lutherans were called to worship on one side of the street and the Presbyterians were called to worship on the other. About fifteen minutes later, the two services became one as bells pealed and the bagpiper began to play. From one side of the street Presbyterians picked up their beautiful wooden sanctuary cross, Communion service, banners, candlesticks, hymnal, and a *Book of Order* and processed into a new era in their life and ministry. On the opposite side of the street the event was just as significant for the Lutherans.

While various forms of shared ministry by congregations of different denominations are not unique in the Presbytery of Prospect Hill, this is the first cooperative ministry between PC(USA) and ELCA congregations in this presbytery since the two denominations adopted a full communion agreement in 1998. The 9,715 members and 59 churches in the presbytery celebrate this response to the critical need for pastoral leadership in rural and small-town communities.

Scripture

What does the LORD your God require of you? Only to fear the LORD your God, to walk in all [the Lord's] ways, to love [the Lord], to serve the LORD your God with all your heart and with all your soul, and to keep the commandments of the LORD your God (Deut. 10:12–13).

Let Us Join in Prayer for:

Presbytery Staff
Rev. James Sanders, executive presbyter
Rev. Nancy Ross-Hullinger, camp administrator
Rev. Randy Knuth, acting stated clerk
J. Jay Wilkinson, treasurer
Darlene Shearer, administrative assistant
Renee Sand, accounting assistant
JoAnn Selleck, resource librarian

PC(USA) General Assembly Staff
Frances Cook, NMD
Rev. Gary Cook, WMD

Daily Lectionary

Ps. 22, 105, 130, 148
Deut. 10:12-22; Heb. 4:11-16
John 3:22-36

Let Us Join in Prayer for:

Presbytery Staff
Rev. Peter B. Funch, executive presbyter
Elder Evelyn Reynen, stated clerk
Carol Iverson, presbytery administrator

PC(USA) General Assembly Staff
Bonnie Cormican, DEDO
Elder Catherine Cottingham, DEDO
Michael Cousins, BOP

THE PRESBYTERY OF SOUTH DAKOTA

South Dakota Presbyterians have a strong connection with the land. That connection is felt most keenly by the farmers and ranchers who make their living from the land, but even residents of the towns and cities across the state feel an attachment to the natural world around them.

While the Presbyterians who live in South Dakota feel that connection, they don't often get the chance to share it with others, to tell others how the animals and plants of the prairies—and they themselves—are part of God's plan.

That's why the opportunity to host a mission trip is so important to small, western South Dakota churches like Bison First Presbyterian and First Presbyterian of Marcus. After the devastating winter of 1996–97, a Volunteer in Mission team from Pennsylvania came to help mend fences for ranchers. While the extra help was appreciated, one rancher summed it up best at the time when he said, "I don't care about my fences, but it sure helped my heart."

The opportunity to share both the land and the connectionalism so central to Presbyterianism was welcomed again in the summer of 2002 when a work crew from Texas came to help paint barns, make small repairs to homes, and spruce up the 4-H grounds in the county seat of Bison (population 400). The work team members spent their evenings holding vacation Bible school.

As a whole, the Presbytery of South Dakota is reaching out to those in need in rural areas. A state-wide training session is planned for parish nurses to assist pastors and congregations as they minister to those in need. The presbytery has 9,521 members and 70 churches.

photo courtesy of Bison First Presbyterian Church

Presbyterians from Pennsylvania helped South Dakotans mend fences.

Daily Lectionary
Ps. 31, 43, 143, 149
Deut. 11:18-28
Heb. 5:1-10; John 4:1-26

Scripture
Jesus said to her, "Everyone who drinks of this water will be thirsty again, but those who drink of the water that I will give them will never be thirsty. The water that I will give will become in them a spring of water gushing up to eternal life" (John 4:13–14).

THE LORD'S DAY

MINUTE FOR MISSION
SAN FRANCISCO THEOLOGICAL SEMINARY

I magine a seminary campus mobbed with high school students—with the disciples of old they ask of Jesus: "LORD, teach us to pray." Under the leadership of Mark Yaconelli and Michael Hryniuk and with the support of a grant from the Lilly Endowment, San Francisco Theological

photo by Lonnie Voth

SFTS Youth Ministry and Spirituality Project co-directors Michael Hryniuk (left) and Mark Yaconelli visit with project manager Deborah Arca Mooney.

Seminary (SFTS) has developed an approach to youth ministry that means much to many. This program grounds youth discipleship in intergenerational practices of prayer, discernment, and spiritual companionship.

- In this first year of its new president, pastor-scholar Philip Butin, SFTS—north and south—is developing new strategies for teaching the mind and heart of the Christian faith.
- In a day when cross-cultural experience marks the landscape of California, pray for the Southern campus that gathers a wonderfully balanced, cross-cultural student body.
- In a year when faculty return from studies in Asia, others leave for work in England, and D.Min. pastors prepare around the world from Africa to Australia to Latin America, pray for growth in grace.

Give thanks for a community that says with the psalmist, "[The LORD] did not hide . . . from me, but heard when I cried. . . . All the ends of the earth shall remember and turn to the LORD" (Ps. 22:24, 27).

The Seminary seeks the prayers of all as SFTS seeks to fulfill God's mission of preparing leaders of the faith for the future, here in the United States and around the world.

—Rev. Dr. James G. Emerson, Jr., interim president,
San Francisco Theological Seminary

Prayer

O God, who made of one blood all people to dwell upon this earth, empower your servants as agents of reconciliation and peace who will overcome terrorism of spirit and soul this day. In the name of the Christ who died and rose for all. Amen.

Sunday Lectionary and Hymns

Gen. 17:1–7, 15–16
Deep in the Shadows of the Past
PH 330

Ps. 22:23–31
Lord, Why Have You Forsaken Me
PH 168; PPCS 17

Rom. 4:13–25
Give to the Winds Thy Fears
PH 286; HB 364

Mark 8:31–38
When We Are Tempted to Deny Your Son
PH 86

Daily Lectionary

Ps. 32, 42, 84, 150
Jer. 1:1-10
1 Cor. 3:11-23; Mark 3:31–4:9

Let Us Join in Prayer for:

Elder Gwendolyn L. Martin,
member, GAC
Elder Manley E. Olson, member, GAC

Presbytery Staff
Rev. Judith P. Kolwicz,
executive presbyter
Rev. Richard H. Headen, associate
executive presbyter
Rev. Deborah DeMeester,
associate executive presbyter
Elder Ernest Cutting, stated clerk
Lois Juth, administrative assistant
Anne-Marie du Jong,
administrative assistant
Katie Houge, administrative assistant

PC(USA) General Assembly Staff
Anita Cowherd, WMD
Jennifer Cox, PPC

Daily Lectionary

Ps. 6, 119:73-80, 121, 145
Jer. 1:11-19
Rom. 1:1-15; John 4:27-42

THE PRESBYTERY OF THE TWIN CITIES AREA   *Minnesota, Wisconsin*

Never has it been more evident that we are equally loved in the eyes of God, not for what we have or where we are from, but for who we are—children of God. As we live in fear for our national security, less fortunate countries fear for their security from disease. In hospital wards on the other side of the world, children are dying every day from malaria. God grieves at this injustice.

Malaria is the number one cause of death for children in Africa under five years old, and it kills 700,000 a year on that continent.

Presbyterian Women in the Twin Cities Area is trying to change the future of children in Africa and Asia by sewing mosquito nets for NetWorkers, a joint project with the International Health Ministries of the PC(USA). NetWorkers coordinates with the World Health Organization, UNICEF, and Christian organizations in a commitment to cut malaria in half by 2010. Each year the parasitic disease infects four million and over a million die.

"NetWorkers gives Presbyterian Women yet another opportunity to offer second-mile giving in its outreach mission to the world," says Elder Ann Rock of First Presbyterian Church in Stillwater, Minnesota.

Deacon Helen Reed of Peace Presbyterian Church, St. Louis Park, sews a bed net for children.

Twin Cities Area Presbyterian Women gather at churches to sew the bed nets and other hospital supplies. Funds sent to participating countries are used in part for training women to educate other women about malaria and mosquito net use and to share Christ with each of them. The circle keeps growing with faith and hope as even more learn of Christ's love and more children are protected from this fatal disease.

The Presbytery of the Twin Cities Area has 26,806 members and 71 congregations.

Scripture
Turn, O LORD, save my life; deliver me for the sake of your steadfast love (Ps. 6:4).

The Presbytery of Winnebago

Wisconsin

According to recent statistics, 97 percent of deaf persons are unchurched. This is not because they are a faithless group, but because so few congregations provide ministry to the deaf. Yet they are hungry for the gospel and will travel quite a distance for worship, pastoral care, and community.

With this need in mind, the ecumenical Hands of Christ Deaf Ministry was established in the greater Fox River Valley in September 1997 to provide direct religious services to deaf and hard-of-hearing individuals and families. The Rev. Gisele Berninghaus, an Evangelical Lutheran Church in

The Hands of Christ Deaf Choir, a part of the ecumenical Hands of Christ Deaf Ministry, sing God's praises!

America minister who also holds membership in the Presbytery of Winnebago, was installed as pastor in December 1997. The Evangelical Lutheran Church in America, the Presbytery of Winnebago, the United Church of Christ, the United Methodist Church, and the Episcopal Diocese of Fond du Lac support the ministry with prayers and finances.

To reach as many people as possible, the Hands of Christ Deaf Ministry offers worship services in churches of the various supporting denominations from Green Bay in the north to Fond du Lac in the south throughout the year. Hands of Christ offers pastoral care, fellowship events, Christian education, and vacation Bible school to the deaf community.

In addition, Gisele Berninghaus and the Hands of Christ Deaf Choir often lead worship in hearing congregations. She preaches in sign language and spoken English, the choir signs the anthems, and the hearing congregation experiences God's word in a new way. It is not uncommon to see smiling faces and raised, waving hands (the deaf sign for applause and appreciation) of both the deaf and hearing members of the congregation.

The Presbytery of Winnebago has 41 churches and 8,809 members.

Scripture

For I am not ashamed of the gospel; it is the power of God for salvation to everyone who has faith, to the Jew first and also to the Greek (Rom. 1:16).

Let Us Join in Prayer for:

Elder Winifred A. Drape, member, GAC

Presbytery Staff
Rev. Dr. Lucille Rupe, executive presbyter
Elder Nancy Barczak, associate, administration
Elder RoseAnn Blair, resource center director
Elder Jean Nymoen, interim task group coordinator
Rev. Dr. Michael B. Lukens, stated clerk

PC(USA) General Assembly Staff
Julie Cox, CMD
Carla Coyle, FDN
Amanda Craft, CMD

Daily Lectionary
Ps. 25, 34, 91, 146
Jer. 2:1-13, 29-32
Rom. 1:16-25; John 4:43-54

Let Us Join in Prayer for:

Partners/Ministries
United Protestant Church of Belgium:
Rev. Daniel Vanescote, president
[Belgium]; Evangelical Lutheran Church
of Finland: **Dr. Risto Cantell**, general
secretary; Orthodox Church in Finland:
His Grace John, archbishop of Karelia
and all Finland; Union of Evangelical
Christians–Baptists of Georgia; Reformed
Christian Church in Yugoslavia (Federal
Republic of Yugoslavia): **Bishop István
Csete-Szemesi**; Evangelical Church of the
Augsburg Confession in Austria:
Bishop Dieter Knall; Evangelical Church
of Austria Helvetic Confession: **Rev. Mag.
Peter Karner**, general superintendent

PC(USA) General Assembly Staff
Rev. Robert Craig, CMD
Angell Crawford, WMD
Rev. Edward Craxton, CMD

EUROPE

The Presbyterian Church (U.S.A.) has been deploying mission workers in the former Soviet Union since 1993. One nation in which PC(USA) mission workers have never been assigned is Belarus. There are Christians, however, in Belarus, just as there were in the old Soviet days. As a result of their country's authoritarian political system, however, they face considerable challenges in building relationships with Christians from the outside world.

Recently the Europe Office of the Presbyterian Church (U.S.A.) organized an ecumenical visit to the churches of Belarus. Participants came from the Reformed churches in Hungary and Poland and from the Russian Orthodox Church, the Evangelical Lutheran Church in Russia, and the Presbyterian Church (U.S.A.)

Daily Lectionary

Ps. 5, 27, 51, 147:1-11
Jer. 3:6-18
Rom. 1:(26-27) 28–2:11; John 5:1-18

Scripture

Return, faithless Israel, says the LORD. I will not look on you in anger, for I am merciful, says the LORD; I will not be angry forever (Jer. 3:12).

EUROPE, *continued*

The participants looked for ways in which their respective national churches could build closer links with Orthodox, Roman Catholic, Baptist, Lutheran, and Reformed counterparts in Belarus. While on this important ecumenical visit, the visitors discovered that Belarusian Christians, perhaps motivated in part by their difficult circumstances, already work closely together to address drug addiction, AIDS prevention, Bible translation and distribution, and evangelism.

Each visitor assumed responsibility for follow-up on behalf of his or her national church. The Polish participant, for instance, will work with colleagues to assist the tiny Reformed communities in Minsk. The Presbyterian Church (U.S.A.) participants will work with others in Worldwide Ministries, as well as with congregations, to help ten tiny Lutheran and Reformed congregations establish themselves to the point where they can organize a Lutheran-Reformed Federation inside the Evangelical Lutheran Church in Russia. A PC(USA) mission worker was invited to join the World Council of Churches-organized Belarus Round Table, which coordinates ecumenical support, including support from PC(USA) congregations, for the projects of the Belarusian churches.

Those interested in mission can learn the value of seeing spiritual life in an unfamiliar place with the eyes of Christians from countries and confessional traditions other than one's own.

Those interested in mission in the former Soviet Union can learn the following from the Belarus example:

- the value of seeing spiritual life in an unfamiliar place with the eyes of Christians from countries and confessional traditions other than one's own
- the importance of getting to know the churches that already exist in a place
- the theological indispensability and practical efficiency of coordinating work ecumenically
- the awareness that the Holy Spirit can work in every situation, even the most difficult.

—*Dr. Duncan Hanson, former coordinator for Europe*

Let Us Join in Prayer for:

PC(USA) People in Mission
Lois Caldwell, mission volunteer, mission partnership enabler, interpreter, Worldwide Ministries Division [Russia]; Moscow Protestant Theological Academy [Russia]: **Hannah Chang Kang**, librarian, **Rev. Joseph Kang**, professor

Partners/Ministries
Union of Evangelical Christians-Baptists of the Russian Federation [Russia]: **Rev. Yuri K. Sipko**, president; Evangelical Lutheran Church in Russia and Other States: **Archbishop Georg Kretschmar**; Russian Orthodox Church: **Patriarch Alexi II**, patriarch of all Russia; St. Andrew's Biblical Theological College [Russia]: **Dr. Alexei Bodrov**; Moscow Presbyterian Theological Academy [Russia]: **Dr. Chang Whan Park**, president; Moscow Protestant Chaplaincy [Russia]: **John Calhoun**, pastor; Presbytery Partnership with the Russian Orthodox Church: Presbytery of Yukon

PC(USA) General Assembly Staff
Robyn Craxton, PW
Robert Creech, DEDO

Let Us Join in Prayer for:

Partners/Ministries
Orthodox Autocephalous Church of
Albania: **His Beatitude Anastasios**,
archbishop of Tirana and all Albania;
Albania Bible Society: **Altin Hysi**, general
secretary; Diakonia Agapes; Albanian
Encouragement Project; Bsksh
student ministry

PC(USA) General Assembly Staff
Deborah Cribb-Bagwell, OGA
Linda Crittenden, DEDO
Lindsay Crosby, BOP

Daily Lectionary

Ps. 27, 102, 126, 147:12-20
Jer. 4:9-10, 19-28
Rom. 2:12-24; John 5:19-29

ALBANIA

Albania continues its struggle to recover from the total political and social crises of 1997 and the Kosovo refugee crisis of 1999. The Albanian economy collapsed in 1997 as a result of the pyramid scheme crisis in which more than one-third of the country's gross domestic product was lost and many Albanians lost their homes, savings, and investments. Then, during the war in Kosovo, Albania—a country of only three million citizens—became host to more than 700,000 refugees fleeing Kosovo. Christianity, nevertheless, is flourishing in Albania, and the PC(USA) continues its role as a participant in the development and strengthening of Christian witness in this former atheistic communist country.

Bob and Dalia Baker, PC(USA) people in mission, provided significant leadership in two crucial ministries during their mission work in Albania. Bob Baker served as the administrative director of the Albanian Encouragement Project (AEP), an umbrella organization for all mission workers and mission agencies serving in Albania. As a lawyer, he provided the leadership to help both mission organizations and the Evangelical Churches of Albania regularize their relationships before the Albanian government. He received special recognition from AEP for his outstanding leadership and his servant heart. After teaching school in the United States for thirty years, Dalia Baker taught in the mission school that serves the evangelical community. As a child refugee after World War II, she responded with compassion and understanding to the influx of refugees to Albania. One of her students was accepted at the Fletcher School of International Relations in Boston.

Jack and Susannah Dabney, PC(USA) mission partners through the Reformed Church of America, continue their ministry of mentoring young Albanian Christians and church leaders. They are developing an English-speaking Christian Fellowship of Tirana to help meet the spiritual needs of the growing expatriate community serving governmental, nongovernmental, and business interests in Albania. Jack Dabney teaches regularly in several Christian training programs and institutions.

Total Area: 10,600 sq. mi. (slightly smaller than Maryland). **Population**: 3,510,484. **Languages**: Albanian, Greek. **GDP Per Capita**: $3,000. **Literacy**: 93%. **Religions**: Muslim, Albanian Orthodox, Roman Catholic. **Life Expectancy**: 71.83 years. **Human Development Index Rank**: 85.

Scripture
"Very truly, I tell you, anyone who hears my word and believes [God] who sent me has eternal life, and does not come under judgment, but has passed from death to life" (John 5:24).

BOSNIA

There are an estimated one million unmarked land mines and other unexploded ordnance in Bosnia and Herzegovina. Land mines were at the center of *No Man's Land*, winner of the Academy Award for best foreign film of 2001. The award for this Bosnian film was presented to its director, Danis Tanovic, on March 25, 2002. The Organization for Security and Co-operation in Europe (OSCE) has cited the film as "an artistic piece of excellence that takes a clear position against war and ethnic division," saying "the OSCE is particularly pleased that on this occasion Bosnia and Herzegovia finds world-wide attention in a cultural context rather than in connotations of violence, ethnic hatred, and war criminals."

Total Area: 19,700 sq. mi. (slightly smaller than West Virginia). **Population**: 3,922,205. **Languages**: Croatian, Serbian, Bosnian. **GDP Per Capita**: $1,700. **Literacy**: NA. **Religions**: Muslim, Orthodox, Roman Catholic, Protestant, other. **Life Expectancy**: 71.75 years. **Human Development Index Rank**: NA.

CROATIA

Steve and Michelle Kurtz, people in mission with the Presbyterian Church (U.S.A.) teaching in Osijek, Croatia, describe what happened when Presbyterians from the United States came to Croatia.

The mission team from Cincinnati, Ohio, joined Hungarians in the ruins of a church in Belye/Bilje, near Osijek. Together they sang, "Lord, you have been our dwelling place in all generations . . . from everlasting to everlasting you are God" (Ps. 90). Pastor Aranka Csati-Szabo said in despair but with hope, "This church building has been destroyed in every war in Europe so far."

The congregation in Cincinnati continues to sponsor mission teams in Croatia that teach vacation Bible school, youth camps, and English as a second language. It sponsors local pastoral ministry, too, as partners and co-workers with the Reformed Church. Other congregations have joined in a widening circle of partnership with the church in Croatia.

Total Area: 21,800 sq. mi. (slightly smaller than West Virginia). **Population**: 4,334,142. **Languages**: Croatian, other. **GDP Per Capita**: $5,800. **Literacy**: 97% (Male 99%, Female 95%). **Religions**: Roman Catholic, Orthodox, Muslim, Protestant, other, unknown. **Life Expectancy**: 73.9 years. **Human Development Index Rank**: 46.

Scripture

My God, my God, why have you forsaken me? Why are you so far from helping me, from the words of my groaning? (Ps. 22:1).

Let Us Join in Prayer for:

PC(USA) People in Mission
Evangelical Theological College, Osijek [Croatia]: **Michelle Pamela Kurtz**, teacher, **Rev. Steven Dale Kurtz**, teacher; **Brett Allen McMichael**, occupational therapist for at-risk children, AGAPE [Croatia]

Partners/Ministries
Reformed Church of Croatia: **Rev. Endre Langh**, bishop; Evangelical Theological Seminary [Croatia]: **Damir Spoljaric**, director, **Peter Kuzmic**, president; Christian Information Service [Croatia]: **Boris Peterlin**, director; Agape [Croatia]: **Antal Balog**, director

PC(USA) General Assembly Staff
Mark Crowner, DEDO
Sallie Cuaresma, NMD
Linda Culbertson, BOP

Daily Lectionary
Ps. 22, 105, 130, 148
Jer. 5:1-9
Rom. 2:25–3:18; John 5:30-47

Let Us Join in Prayer for:

PC(USA) People in Mission
Rev. John David Michael, Jr., ecumenical assistant, Evangelical Church of Czech Brethren; **Rev. Joyce Mauler Michael,** translation and editing ministry

Partners/Ministries
Evangelical Church of Czech Brethren: **Rev. Pavel Smetana,** synodal senior; Ecumenical Council of Churches: **Nadeje Mandysova,** director; Foundation Diakonie: **Pavel Vychopen,** director; Protestant Theological Faculty of Charles University: **Professor Thdr Petr Pokorny,** dean; Czech Council of Churches: **Nadeje Mandysova,** general secretary

PC(USA) General Assembly Staff
Rev. Belinda Curry, DEDO
Elder Jean Cutler, PW
Dana Dages, NMD

Daily Lectionary

Ps. 31, 43, 143, 149
Jer. 5:20-31
Rom. 3:19-31; John 7:1-13

CZECH REPUBLIC

The Rev. Blahoslav Hájek of the Evangelical Church of Czech Brethren almost wept one morning during worship. He remembers, "It is not proper, of course, the Sunday worship of the church is a joyful celebration and not a mourning occasion. So I felt a bit uneasy, I did not dare to turn my head round, I only kept my handkerchief and tried to hide my tears.

Still the glory of the Lord is unshaken, and the people recognize God's love in Jesus Christ, just as their predecessors did.

"What was the matter? We sang Psalm 84, 'Blessed are they who dwell within Thy house.' And I suddenly realized that this was exactly the same psalm and these were the same words we sang in the church when my mother was sitting next to me some forty years ago. This time it was my son who was sitting next to me.

"Is that not astonishing? What was happening during these years and decades? How many schools did I go through, how many experiences did I gather, how much skill did I acquire in the meantime? How many people have gone, how many young people have grown up in the meantime? How much technology have we introduced? How many changes has my country gone through? How much atheistic teaching has been taught in the meantime, how much atheistic behavior surrounds us nowadays? But the word of God remains forever, and the people confess God steadfastly.

"They cannot be the same, the conditions of life do change, even they themselves live and think differently from the way their fathers and mothers did. But still the glory of the Lord is unshaken, and the people recognize God's love in Jesus Christ, just as their predecessors did. Praise be to the Lord as it was at the beginning, as it is now, and as it will be forever!"

Total Area: 30,300 sq. mi. (slightly smaller than South Carolina). **Population**: 10,264,212. **Languages**: Czech. **GDP Per Capita**: $12,900. **Literacy**: 99.9%. **Religions**: atheist, Roman Catholic, Protestant, Orthodox, other. **Life Expectancy**: 74.73 years. **Human Development Index Rank**: 33.

Scripture

For there is no distinction, since all have sinned and fall short of the glory of God; they are now justified by [God's] grace as a gift, through the redemption that is in Christ Jesus (Rom. 3:22–24).

THE LORD'S DAY

MINUTE FOR MISSION
YOUNG PEOPLE IN THE CHURCH

Bump, bump went the car along the Pennsylvania Turnpike. Delegates from the Presbytery of Baltimore headed home from the very first Connection Assembly, Connection 97, a youth General Assembly. They were exhausted, yet exhilarated because this was a new and exciting way in which to minister to youth. For the next two years, the Presbytery of Baltimore put into practice what was learned at Connection 97. One decision made at the Assembly was to begin a Youth Council. Two-thirds of the Council's membership are youth and one-third are adults. The Youth Council plans and implements two youth retreats and a Connection Rally each year.

Youth participate in the 2002 Connection Rally, whose theme was "You are not the weakest link."

The Youth Council spent two years planning the first Connection Rally, held in 2000. Then churches and youth brought forth legislation that was worked through in committees and then voted on by the assembled youth. Three overtures were approved at the rally, one each on updating the *Guidebook for Youth Ministry*, creating a resource for training youth to become peacemakers, and asking the General Assembly to be intentional about placing youth on standing committees. At the Rally, delegates were elected to attend the 2000 Connection Assembly. The 2001 Rally produced a connection report, conducted workshops, and commissioned Triennium delegates.

At the Connection Rally in 2002, youth received the Triennium report, enjoyed workshops, and listened to keynote speaker Andrew Buckley, program assistant for the Office of Youth Ministry, and the first male Presbyterian Youth Connection co-moderator. The 2003 Rally will feature youth-generated legislation from the seventy-two churches of the Presbytery of Baltimore.

We are blessed as God works through the youth of our denomination.

—Rev. Mark Sandell, member, Presbytery of Baltimore Youth Council

Prayer

Gracious God, we praise you for the fresh wind that is blowing across youth ministry within the Presbyterian Church (U.S.A.). May you continue to express your love through those who work with youth. Let us not judge others based on what they wear, how they look, or how old they are. Rather, let us enjoy the gifts and talents you have given to the church in the form of our youth. In Jesus' name, Amen.

Sunday Lectionary and Hymns

Exod. 20:1–17
God Marked a Line and Told the Sea
PH 283

Ps. 19
Joyful, Joyful, We Adore Thee
PH 464; HB 21; PPCS 12

1 Cor. 1:18–25
In the Cross of Christ I Glory
PH 84; HB 195

John 2:13–22
With Joy I Heard My Friends Exclaim
PH 235; HB 439

Daily Lectionary

Ps. 32, 42, 84, 150
Jer. 6:9-15
1 Cor. 6:12-20; Mark 5:1-20

BRITAIN/IRELAND

Let Us Join in Prayer for:

PC(USA) People in Mission
Rev. Thomas Joseph Arthur, pastor,
United Reformed Church; St. Helens,
Church of England: **Kenneth Dale Davis**,
community worker, **Stephanie Ann Davis**,
community worker; Time For God young
adult volunteers, church/community
workers: **Tara Elizabeth Ebner**, **Kurt W.
Esslinger**, **Jonathan Scott Hauerwas**,
and **Allison Lea Rasa**

Partners/Ministries
Church of Scotland: **Very Rev. Finlay
MacDonald**, principal clerk; Iona
Community [Scotland]: **Rev. Norman
Shanks**, leader

PC(USA) General Assembly Staff
Thomas Daly III, BOP
Jane Daveler, BOP
Elder April Davenport, EDO

Ann Stephan Davis and Kenneth Dale Davis have ministered to Bengali and Pakistani Muslims in East London, England, for a number of years. They now live in the village of Sutton, from where they are coordinating the Homework Helpers tutoring program throughout the United Kingdom. This program links volunteer Christian tutors with Asian Muslim children, who, by helping them with their homework, are witnessing to the gospel of Jesus Christ.

This program links volunteer Christian tutors with Asian Muslim children, who, by helping them with their homework, are witnessing to the gospel of Jesus Christ.

The General Assembly of the Church of Scotland, according to the Rev. Ian Alexander, assistant secretary for the Middle East and Europe, has received a report from a special commission on the need to encourage review and reform in the national church. Titled "A Church without Walls," the report calls members back to the simple challenge of Jesus—"follow me." Mr. Alexander notes that while the Church of Scotland, like many other churches, is declining in membership, "It has been marvelous to see God's spirit beginning to move in powerful ways again in our land as a result of people grappling with the issues raised in this significant report. A team of advisers in mission and evangelism has encouraged congregations to look at six major issues contained in the report, which congregations have to wrestle with if we are once again going to become vibrant communities of love, service, and fellowship." These major issues are transforming the local congregation, the spiritual journey, following Jesus today, partnerships, the ministry of the whole people, and eldership/leadership.

Mr. Alexander says, "Many painful decisions remain to be taken—we probably still have too many old church buildings in our country. But at last the Christians here in Scotland are grappling with these very challenging issues."

> **GREAT BRITAIN**
> **U.K. Total Area**: 93,200 sq. mi. (slightly smaller than Oregon). **Population**: 59,647,790. **Languages**: English, Welsh, Scottish form of Gaelic. **GDP Per Capita**: $22,800. **Literacy**: 99%. **Religions**: Anglican, Roman Catholic, Muslim, Presbyterian, Methodist, Sikh, Hindu, Jewish. **Life Expectancy**: 77.82 years. **Human Development Index Rank**: 14.

Daily Lectionary

Ps. 6, 119:73-80, 121, 145
Jer. 7:1-15
Rom. 4:1-12; John 7:14-36

Scripture

Now to one who works, wages are not reckoned as a gift but as something due. But to one who without works trusts [God] who justifies the ungodly, such faith is reckoned as righteousness (Rom. 4:4–5).

Britain/Ireland, *continued*

Fortwilliam Presbyterian Church is located in a part of North Belfast that has rapidly been becoming predominantly Catholic. Nevertheless, the members of the congregation believe it is important to continue where they are and use their building to serve the whole community.

One February night when PC(USA) Young Adult Volunteer Beth Cooke arrived to prepare for the youth fellowship meeting, she discovered that the church had been broken into and several electrical items stolen—ranging from a microwave and CD players to part of the new public address system. For the staff and members it was difficult to cope with the mess, and Fortwilliam was already operating on a minimum of resources. However, the amount of support that poured in was truly unexpected. Lesley Carroll, the minister, had 150 messages on her answering machine; scores of letters and cards arrived, and people sent gifts of money. Replacement TVs and music centers were sent and the center was offered PA systems, installed, and on free loan.

Lesley Carroll recalled, "At the time it felt like a kick in the teeth. . . . But Tracy Magee from Ulster TV put it in perspective for me when she said, 'So this is really an attack on the whole community and not just on your church?' The answer of course was 'yes' because our halls are used daily by the community."

Two local Catholic schools called early the next day to offer work parties to help with the clean-up. This was only the beginning of the support offered by Fortwilliam's neighbors, who recognize that the church is helping the whole community.

Lesley Carroll said, "For me, our mission has been affirmed. We are in fact better off now in knowing we belong to the wider church and knowing our place in the community."

IRELAND
Total Area: 26,600 sq. mi. (slightly larger than West Virginia). **Population**: 3,840,838. **Languages**: English, Irish (Gaelic). **GDP Per Capita**: $21,600. **Literacy**: 98%. **Religions**: Roman Catholic, Church of Ireland, other. **Life Expectancy**: 76.99 years. **Human Development Index Rank**: 18.

Scripture
O taste and see that the LORD is good; happy are those who take refuge in [the Lord] (Ps. 34:8).

Let Us Join in Prayer for:

PC(USA) People in Mission
Presbyterian Church in Ireland: **Laura Renn Crim**, young adult volunteer, youth and community ministry intern, **Elisabeth Burns Hatch**, mission volunteer, youth worker, **Carol Renee Puckett**, young adult volunteer, youth and community ministry intern, **Mark Allan Zimmerly**, young adult volunteer, youth and community ministry intern, Presbyterian Church in Ireland; Mediation Network of Northern Ireland: **Rev. Douglas Reid Baker**, peacemaking advocacy, **Margaret Elaine Baker**, team ministry

Partners/Ministries
Presbyterian Church in Ireland: **Rev. Donald Watts**, clerk of the assembly, general secretary; Irish School of Ecumenics: **Dr. Geraldine Smyth**, director; Corrymeela Community: **Trevor Williams**, leader; Mediation Network; Nexus Lucan Youth Centre [Rep. of Ireland]: **Maurice** and **Helen Kennedy**, administrators; United Reformed Church [England]: **The Rev. Dr. David Cornick**, general secretary; Church of England; United Reformed Church [England]: **Rev. Anthony G. Burnham**, general secretary; Time for God [England]

PC(USA) General Assembly Staff
Diane Davenport, BOP
Kathleen Davenport, BOP

Daily Lectionary
Ps. 25, 34, 91, 146
Jer. 7:21-34
Rom. 4:13-25; John 7:37-52

Let Us Join in Prayer for:

Partners/Ministries
Reformed Church in Alsace-Lorraine: **Antoine Pfeiffer**, president of the synodal council; Protestant Federation of France: **Christian Seytre**, general secretary; Reformed Church of France: **Rev. Marc Richalot**, general secretary, **Rev. Marcel Manoël**, president; Federation of Evangelical Churches in France; Evangelical Community for Apostolic Action; L'Année Diaconale; Church of the Augsburg Confession: **Rev. Michel Hoeffel**, president; CIMADE: **Genevieve Jacques**, general secretary; Uniting Protestant Churches in the Netherlands

PC(USA) General Assembly Staff
Deborah Davies, OGA
Gloria Davis, BOP
Teresa Day, DEDO

Daily Lectionary

Ps. 5, 27, 51, 147:1-11
Jer. 8:4-7, 18–9:6
Rom. 5:1-11; John 8:12-20

FRANCE

In a public address to the citizens of France, President Jacques Chirac declared, "When a synagogue is burned it is France that is humiliated; when a Jew is assaulted it is France that is assaulted." The aura of hatred generated by prolonged heightened tension in the Middle East in the spring of 2002 led to alarming acts of anti-Semitism in France. Synagogues were vandalized and burned. In retaliation, pro-Israeli slogans were scrawled on the walls of Arab-owned businesses. "Passions that flare up in the Middle East must not flare up here," Prime Minister Lionel Jospin said. "We must not import this violence."

President Chirac remained unswerving in his condemnation of race- and religion-related acts of hatred and in his assertion that the French Republic has "the obligation of respect, tolerance, and dialogue with regard to the freedom of thought, the freedom of expression, and religious freedom."

Total Area: 210,400 sq. mi. (slightly less than twice the size of Colorado). **Population**: 59,551,227. **Languages**: French, rapidly declining regional dialects and languages. **GDP Per Capita**: $24,400. **Literacy**: 99%. **Religions**: Roman Catholic, Protestant, Jewish, Muslim, unaffiliated. **Life Expectancy**: 78.9 years. **Human Development Index Rank**: 13.

NETHERLANDS

Laurens Hogebrink, a Dutch Reformed pastor, manages the European and North American office of the Uniting Protestant Churches in the Netherlands, a merger of the Lutheran church and the two main Reformed churches, the largest Dutch Protestant church.

Pastor Hogebrink explains that the merging process is not easy, nationally or locally. "Becoming one church involves overcoming differences in tradition and structure. However, there is already much cooperation.

"Congregations in the Netherlands and churches in Central and Eastern Europe began partnerships during the Cold War as an expression of Christian solidarity with sisters and brothers living under communism. When the Berlin Wall fell in 1989 some eight hundred church partnerships existed."

Today many such alliances continue, encouraging ecumenism and integration within a unifying Europe and exploring the role of the church in European society.

Total Area: 13,100 sq. mi. (slightly less than twice the size of New Jersey). **Population**: 15,981,472. **Languages**: Dutch. **GDP Per Capita**: $24,400. **Literacy**: 99%. **Religions**: Roman Catholic, Protestant, Muslim, other, unaffiliated. **Life Expectancy**: 78.43 years. **Human Development Index Rank**: 8.

Scripture

Therefore, since we are justified by faith, we have peace with God through our LORD Jesus Christ (Rom. 5:1).

GERMANY

Berlin is a city with 3.4 million inhabitants. Decades ago it was a Protestant city in which more than 70 percent of the population belonged to the Lutheran Church. Ongoing secularization and the Communist government have reduced the membership to 30 percent. But this does not mean that the church is truly a fading church. The Rev. Hans-Georg Filker, director of the Evangelical Mission Society in Germany, says, "No! Mission is possible!" There is an urgent need for evangelization and social assistance. As a sign of hope the Berlin City Mission is establishing a Christian Urban Center in the heart of the city. It will include a guest house with about two hundred beds, social programs, the planting of a local mission church, and outreach to urban people. Land is available adjacent to a new railway station where in a few years more than 300,000 passengers are expected daily. This mission will invite urban people—the homeless, the elderly, and the poor as well as the rich—to hear and respond to the gospel, and it will be a challenge to bring the gospel to the postmodern world.

Total Area: 135,100 sq. mi. (slightly smaller than Montana). **Population**: 83,029,536. **Language**: German. **GDP Per Capita**: $23,400. **Religions**: Protestant, Roman Catholic, Muslim, unaffiliated or other. **Literacy**: 99%. **Life Expectancy**: 77.61 years. **Human Development Index Rank**: 17.

GREECE

The 2004 Summer Olympic Games that will be held in August in Athens, Greece, are providing an impetus for launching an Olympic truce. With the motto, "On your marks, ready—cease-fire," the truce is directed toward a sixteen-day period of peace around the world. The idea stems from the days of ancient Greece, when parties at war suspended conflicts during the Olympics so that the warriors could take part in the games. Foreign Minister George Papandreou, vice-president of the International Olympic Truce Center, said, "The goal is that every time there are Olympics, this principle will be respected more and more." The center was founded under the auspices of the International Olympic Committee.

Total Area: 50,400 sq. mi. (slightly smaller than Alabama). **Population**: 10,623,835. **Languages**: Greek (official), English, French. **GDP Per Capita**: $17,200. **Literacy**: 95% (Male 98%, Female 93%). **Religions**: Greek Orthodox, Muslim, other. **Life Expectancy**: 78.59 years. **Human Development Index Rank**: 23.

Scripture

Correct me, O Lord, but in just measure; not in your anger, or you will bring me to nothing (Jer. 10:24).

Let Us Join in Prayer for:

PC(USA) People in Mission
Black Forest Academy [Germany]: **James Thomas Adams**, school administrator, **Nancy Joy Adams**, school administrator and teacher; Evangelical Church in Berlin-Brandenburg [Germany]: **Rev. Gregory K. Callison**, evangelist, Kurdish refugees, **Rev. Christine Ruth Goodman-Callison**, pastor, evangelism and church growth among Kurds; **Burkhard Paetzold**, Roma ministry consultant, Jinishian Memorial Program [Germany]; **Azizollah Sadaghiani**, refugee worker, Iranian Presbyterian Fellowship in Europe [Germany]; **Rev. Sadegh Mohammad Sepehri Fard**, refugee worker, Berliner Missionswerk [Germany]

Partners/Ministries
Berliner Stadtmission [Germany]: **Rev. Hans-Georg Filker**, director; Evangelical Church in Berlin-Brandenburg [Germany]: **Bishop Wolfgang Huber**; Evangelical Church of Germany; Evangelical Church of the Union [Germany]: **Bishop Dr. Martin Kruse**, general secretary; Berlin Mission Society [Germany]: **Rev. Ekkehard Zipser**, director; Berlin City Mission [Germany]: **Rev. Hans-Georg Filker**, director; Evangelical Mission Society in Germany: **Rev. Herbert Meissner**, general secretary; Greek Evangelical Church: **Rev. Phaedon Cambouropoulos**, general secretary

PC(USA) General Assembly Staff
Kimberly Deaton, DEDO

Daily Lectionary

Ps. 27, 102, 126, 147:12-20
Jer. 10:11-24
Rom. 5:12-21; John 8:21-32

Let Us Join in Prayer for:

PC(USA) People in Mission
Reformed Church of Hungary (RCH):
Rev. Kathleen E. Andress-Angi, facilitator, psycho-social and children's work, **Joseph A. Angi**, team ministry, **Rev. Ruth Kaeja Cho**, pastor, Korean Cultural and Mission Center, **Rev. Stephen Soo-Kyung Cho**, ministry assistant, Korean Cultural and Mission Center

Partners/Ministries
RCH: **Rev. Gustáv Bölcskei**, presiding bishop, **Rev. Bertalan Tamás**, ecumenical officer; Balatonszarszo Conference Center; Korean Mission and Cultural Center; Hungarian Interchurch Aid; Bethesda Children's Hospital; Immanuel Home; Presbytery Partnerships with the RCH: Missouri Union Presbytery, and the Presbytery of the Twin Cities Area

PC(USA) General Assembly Staff
Nancy Deeney, BOP
Rev. Jaime Delgado, CMD
Trina Deluca, BOP

Daily Lectionary

Ps. 22, 105, 130, 148
Jer. 11:1-8, 14-17
Rom. 6:1-11; John 8:33-47

HUNGARY

The Presbyterian Church (U.S.A.) is represented in Hungary by the Rev. Ruth Kaeja Cho and the Rev. Stephen Soo-Kyung Cho, who have been serving the Roma people for the past five years.

Kathy and Joe Angi are also part of the Presbyterian presence in Hungary. Kathy Angi is the first mission co-worker assigned to be a field presence for Presbyterian Disaster Assistance. Communicating about their work, they write: "Responding with compassion to people who are refugees is a mission direction chosen by the Reformed Church in Hungary. Within Hungary's borders are as many as 3,000 refugees in temporary camps at any given moment. People wait here for coveted asylum status or visas to a country that will accept them, giving them a desperately needed new beginning. The wait can be for weeks or years, living in a legal abyss that does not allow them to have jobs, pursue an education, or travel freely.

Kaeja Cho gathers with Roma children after a youth meeting.

"This period of waiting is the focus of the church's ministry. How might the church reach out to fellow human beings while they wait? What resources do the people of the Hungarian Reformed Churches have that might be shared with these visitors to their country? Many people in Hungary are themselves struggling to move beyond basic survival living. . . . Involving lay people in mission is a new direction for the church here. During the years of communism, church membership often precipitated harassment, and church activity was actively suppressed. As the church emerges from this history, the memories linger and interfere with the present and future life of the church."

Total Area: 35,600 sq. mi. (slightly smaller than Indiana). **Population**: 10,106,017. **Languages**: Hungarian, other. **GDP Per Capita**: $11,200. **Literacy**: 99%. **Religions**: Roman Catholic, Calvinist, Lutheran, atheist, other. **Life Expectancy**: 71.63 years. **Human Development Index Rank**: 36.

Scripture

Therefore we have been buried with [Christ] by baptism into death, so that, just as Christ was raised from the dead by the glory of the Father, so we too might walk in newness of life (Rom. 6:4).

ITALY

*C*onfronti, meaning face-to-face dialogue or comparison—not confrontation—is an interfaith ministry and magazine," write PC(USA) people in mission Michele and Terry Finseth, who focus on Muslim-Christian relations in Confronti, working in partnership with the Waldensian Church in Rome, Italy. They note that "dialogue is a key concept in Italy, where society is becoming more and more pluralistic in culture and faith. Dialogue can become the catalyst to knock down the walls of fear, mistrust, and fundamentalism and build bridges of true mutual understanding." One of the international programs, Seeds of Peace in Kosovo, is an educational and training program designed to support intercultural dialogue and foster a sense of community among the Serbians, Albanians, Askalija, Roma, Gorans, Turks, and Bosnians who live there.

Children are involved in therepeutic play activity as part of the Seeds of Peace program.

The Finseths developed an interethnic after-school program and summer camp for children with disabilities (and nondisabled children) between the ages of six and fourteen, in an effort to overcome the traumas of warfare and ethnic violence. They also held training courses for their teachers in nonviolent conflict management, first with individual ethnic groups in Kosovo and then in an interethnic course in Italy with a follow-up in Macedonia.

The teachers were committed to the courses, which took place during the conflict and even while some of their own relatives were being discovered buried in mass graves. Many received threats for participating in a course with the "enemy." Once the teachers were removed from the environment of ethnic hatred, Michele and Terry Finseth say, it was exciting to watch the transformation experience as they bonded with one another during the two-week seminar.

Total Area: 113,400 sq. mi. (slightly larger than Arizona). **Population**: 57,679,825. **Languages**: Italian (official), German, French, Slovene. **GDP Per Capita**: $22,100. **Literacy**: 98%. **Religions**: Roman Catholic, Protestant, Jewish, Muslim. **Life Expectancy**: 79.14 years. **Human Development Index Rank**: 20.

Scripture

For the wages of sin is death, but the free gift of God is eternal life in Christ Jesus our LORD *(Rom. 6:23).*

Let Us Join in Prayer for:

PC(USA) People in Mission
Waldensian Evangelical Church:
Michele Reed Finseth, team ministry,
Terry Arnold Finseth,
Muslim-Christian relations

Partners/Ministries
Waldensian Evangelical Church:
Rev. Gianni Genre, moderator; Confronti:
Rev. Paolo Naso, director; Waldensian Theological Seminary; Federation of Evangelical Churches in Italy: **Anne-Marie Dupre**, Refugee and Migrant Service; Casa Materna: **Rosaria Vincenzi**, administrator; Presbytery Partnership with the Waldensian/Methodist Church: Presbytery of Beaver-Butler

PC(USA) General Assembly Staff
Linda Denning, FDN
Sheldon Dennis, BOP
Terry Dennis, BOP

Daily Lectionary

Ps. 31, 43, 143, 149
Jer. 13:1-11
Rom. 6:12-23; John 8:47-59

Sunday Lectionary and Hymns

Num. 21:4–9
There Is a Balm in Gilead
PH 394

Ps. 107:1–3, 17–22
We Thank You, Lord, for You Are Good
PH 243; PPCS 109, 110

Eph. 2:1–10
When I Had Not Yet Learned of Jesus
PH 410

John 3:14–21
I Greet Thee, Who My Sure Redeemer Art
PH 457; HB 144

THE LORD'S DAY

MINUTE FOR MISSION
SELF-DEVELOPMENT OF PEOPLE

Today is the churchwide celebration of the Self-Development of People ministry. For nearly thirty-three years, thousands of church volunteers and staff serving national, synod, and presbytery Self-Development of People committees, and their ecumenical partners, have devoted their efforts to helping the economically poor, oppressed, and disadvantaged people for whom Christ came move toward the abundant life.

Over those years, the ministry has focused its efforts on helping people gain control over their own lives, such as with the Yu Chow farmers' water project in Henan Province, China. With the help of Self-Development of People, villagers turned barren soil into verdant farmland and found ways to bring life-giving water

Self-Development of People helps villagers turn barren soil into verdant farmland.

into their village homes. Mothers formerly on welfare in Washington, California, and New Mexico have gained self-respect and the respect of others as they have worked for new lives for themselves and their families. Thousands of people in hundreds of other small, community-owned projects in places like Brazil, Egypt, Ghana, Argentina, Guatemala, Uganda, Dominican Republic, Kenya, and the United States have been able to carry out projects that have improved the quality of their lives. Self-Development church volunteers, staff, and ecumenical partners have grown and developed as well. They have broadened their friendships, learned from people with whom they have interacted, and emerged from these relationships with a greater harmony with God and God's creation. They have lived out the Self-Development of People.

—*Dr. Fredric T. Walls, former director, Self-Development of People*

Prayer
Loving God, we thank you for Jesus Christ, who came that all people would have abundant life. By your Spirit, help us to continue to stand with and support our sisters and brothers who have been oppressed by poverty. Help us, in whatever we say and do, to follow Jesus' example and to have his mind in us, so that we may live and work to help restore your plan for your people and your creation. In Christ's name. Amen.

Daily Lectionary

Ps. 32, 42, 84, 150
Jer. 14:1-9 (10-16) 17-22
Gal. 4:21–5:1; Mark 8:11-21

LITHUANIA

The road to recovery from Soviet occupation is not an easy one. Lithuania is struggling to reestablish itself economically, politically, and spiritually. This is the setting in which Lithuania Christian College (LCC) contributes to the restoration of hope and trust. As a Christian liberal arts college, LCC is unique in the Baltic states. The role of LCC is affirmed by the mission statement that directs its purpose: Lithuania Christian College provides university education within an international learning community that transforms people for servant leadership. Jane Holslag, Jackie Bartz, and Eric and Becky Hinderliter represent the PC(USA) at the college. They contribute to the role of the college as a voice for a Christian worldview and participate in its work as an international community affirming human dignity.

Total Area: 25,100 sq. mi. (slightly larger than West Virginia). Population: 3,610,535. Languages: Lithuanian (official), Polish, Russian. GDP Per Capita: $7,300. Literacy: 98% (Male 99%, Female 98%). Religions: Roman Catholic, Lutheran, Russian Orthodox, Protestant, Evangelical Christian Baptist, Muslim, Jewish. Life Expectancy: 69.25 years. Human Development Index Rank: 47.

POLAND

The Evangelical Reformed Church of Poland (ERCP) is celebrating the opening of a new conference center and guesthouse in Pstrazna, near the border with Czechoslavakia. Dr. Joanna J. Mizgala of the ERCP writes about the role the center will play for this 4,000-member denomination. "First, it will provide a space to study, pray, and rest for members of our church who ordinarily would not even meet, living their everyday existence far from each other and often far from the nearest Reformed congregation. With Pstrazna near the Czech border we also envision the center as a place for international ecumenical guests to spend some time in a relaxed atmosphere, sharing their Christian witness with their Polish counterparts. We appreciate the prayers of the PC(USA) family for the new bishop, the consistory, the presbyters, and all members of our church."

Total Area: 117,400 sq. mi. (slightly smaller than New Mexico). Population: 38,633,912. Language: Polish. GDP Per Capita: $8,500. Literacy: 99%. Religions: Roman Catholic, Eastern Orthodox, Protestant, other. Life Expectancy: 73.42 years. Human Development Index Rank: 38.

Scripture
"Therefore I am surely going to teach them, this time I am going to teach them my power and my might, and they shall know that my name is the LORD" (Jer. 16:21).

Let Us Join in Prayer for:

PC(USA) People in Mission
Lithuania Christian College (LCC): **Jacquelin Ann Bartz**, mission volunteer, English teacher, **Dr. Eric L. Hinderliter**, coordinator, Micro Enterprise Center, economics teacher, **Rebecca A. Hinderliter**, team ministry, **Rev. Jane Holslag**, instructor, theology and English; **Duncan Hanson**, board member

Partners/Ministries
Reformed Christian Church in Lithuania; Faculty of Klaipeda University [Lithuania]: **Arunas Baublys**, dean; LCC: **Jim Mininger**, president; Presbytery Partnership with the Evangelical Reformed Church of Lithuania: Mission Presbytery; Evangelical Church-Augsburg Confession [Poland]: **Bishop Jan Szarek**; Evangelical Reformed Church of Poland: **Marek Izdebsui**, bishop, **Witold Brodzínki**, president of the consistory

PC(USA) General Assembly Staff
Elder Lionel Derenoncourt, WMD
Elder John Detterick, EDO
Brenda Devine, WMD

Daily Lectionary
Ps. 6, 119:73-80, 121, 145
Jer. 16:(1-9) 10-21
Rom. 7:1-12; John 6:1-15

Let Us Join in Prayer for:

PC(USA) People in Mission
Spanish Evangelical Church: **Rev. Donna L. Moros**, co-principal (theological instructor), **Dr. Rev. Edgar Roberto Moros-Ruano**, co-principal (theological instructor); **Rev. Bryce Little** and **Phyllis Little** regional facilitators, Spain and Portugal

Partners/Ministries
Evangelical Presbyterian Church in Portugal; Spanish Evangelical Church: **Rev. Alfredo Abad**, general secretary; United Evangelical Theological Seminary [Spain]: **Dr. Pedro Zamora**, co-director, **Rogelio Prieto**, co-director

PC(USA) General Assembly Staff
Anne Devlin, BOP
Shari Devonish, MSS
Rev. Arthur J. DeYoung, CMD

Daily Lectionary

Ps. 25, 34, 91, 146
Jer. 17:19-27
Rom. 7:13-25; John 6:16-27

PORTUGAL

Since its inception in 1838, the Presbyterian Church of Portugal has been ministering to the spiritual and physical needs of suffering, poor, and socially excluded people. In Cova e Gala, a fishing village struggling with the effects of community-wide unemployment, Portuguese Presbyterians have joined with the inhabitants to create a haven of security and stability for village youth. Congregations from Cova e Gala and neighboring Figueira da Foz, pastored by the Rev. Andreas Ding, created the aZone (alternative zone) where children ages 7 to 16 acquire self-esteem and self-confidence through sports, music, art, computer training, and summer camps. He reports that "the aZone is growing: we have been asked to start activities in a neighboring village and to give training courses in two Presbyterian congregations that would like to begin a similar ministry."

Total Area: 35,300 sq. mi. (slightly smaller than Indiana). **Population**: 10,066,253. **Language**: Portuguese. **GDP Per Capita**: $15,800. **Literacy**: 87.4%. **Religions**: Roman Catholic, Protestant. **Life Expectancy**: 75.94 years. **Human Development Index Rank**: 28.

SPAIN

The Rev. Dr. Edgar Moros-Ruano and the Rev. Donna Laubach Moros are people in mission invited by the Evangelical Church of Spain and the Reformed Episcopal Church of Spain to work at the Seminario Evangelico Unído de Téologia, which opened its own campus in El Escorial in 2002. They write, "After many years of struggle, this southern European seminary, representing the Protestant religious minority, is a survivor of many years of discrimination and dislocation. It lived through the Spanish Civil War and then was violently shut down by the Franco regime. Over the years it has moved through five different buildings and cities. We are all very hopeful about the new phase. This is also exciting for our own PC(USA) as a denomination, which has held a very important role in helping this institution to resist repression and remain alive. We can be proud of our presence here. It is a partnership with deep roots."

Total Area: 192,600 sq. mi. (slightly more than twice the size of Oregon). **Population**: 40,037,995. **Languages**: Castilian Spanish (official), Catalan, Galician, Basque. **GDP Per Capita**: $18,000. **Literacy**: 97%. **Religions**: Roman Catholic, other. **Life Expectancy**: 78.93 years. **Human Development Index Rank**: 21.

Scripture

O magnify the LORD with me, and let us exalt [the Lord's] name together (Ps. 34:3).

ROMANIA

Homelessness in Romania is an ever-increasing problem, and there are only a handful of private homeless shelters with which to work. How can one PC(USA) missionary English teacher help where help is really needed?" asks Lisa Lumpp, a mission volunteer in Romania. "Alone, I simply don't have the resources. If not for [your] contributions and support, we would not have been able to accomplish all that we have. Together, we have provided funds for books to the local Reformed high school; brought fun and games with teachings of Christ to neighborhood children and an orphanage; helped a local ecumenical Bible study group think about what it means to be open and tolerant; and taught English to some outstanding kids! Recently we learned that 16 percent of the students at the Reformed high school in Satu Mare have a working knowledge of English, compared to 8 percent last year. So, together we are making progress!"

Total Area: 88,800 sq. mi. (slightly smaller than Oregon). **Population**: 22,364,022. **Languages**: Romanian, Hungarian, German. **GDP Per Capita**: $5,900. **Literacy**: 97% (Male 98%, Female 95%). **Religions**: Romanian Orthodox, Roman Catholic, Uniate Catholic, Protestant, unaffiliated. **Life Expectancy**: 70.16 years. **Human Development Index Rank**: 58.

SLOVAKIA

The Rev. John Michael, mission specialist in Slovakia, reports that during the communist era in the former Czechoslovakia, public service organizations, including church-related diaconal organizations, were forbidden. However, immediately following the Velvet Revolution of 1989 almost all of the churches in the country began various forms of public service. In need of such service, Roma people face problems that seem nearly insoluble. The church in the Czech Republic, however, has begun to address these problems and is making the education of Roma children a priority.

In the town of Pardubice, the Ecumenical Council of Churches (ECC) found a school principal with whom to work to set up a preschool for Roma children. Additionally, the ECC provided a member of the Evangelical Church of Czech Brethren to serve as a teacher.

Total Area: 18,800 sq. mi. (about twice the size of New Hampshire). **Population**: 5,414,937. **Languages**: Slovak (official), Hungarian. **GDP Per Capita**: $10,200. **Literacy**: NA. **Religions**: Roman Catholic, atheist, Protestant, Orthodox, other. **Life Expectancy**: 73.97 years. **Human Development Index Rank**: 35.

Scripture

"Come, go down to the potter's house, and there I will let you hear my words" (Jer. 18:2).

Let Us Join in Prayer for:

PC(USA) People in Mission
Mary K. Ferris, youth and children's worker, Orphans, Relief & Aid International (ORA) [Romania]

Partners/Ministries
Reformed Church in Romania; Reformed Church of Romania, Clui Diocese: **Bishop Geza Pap**; Reformed Church of Romania, Oradea Diocese: **Bishop László Tökes**; Casuta Noastra Orphanage [Romania]; United Protestant Theological Institute [Romania]; Ecumenical Association of Churches in Romania-Aidrom: **Christian Teodorescu**, executive secretary; Presbytery Partnership with the Reformed Church in Romania: Flint River Presbytery and the Lehigh Presbytery; Reformed Church of Slovakia: **Géza Erdélyi**, bishop; Church of the Brethren in the Slovak Republic: **Ing. Ondrej Kerekréty**, general secretary

PC(USA) General Assembly Staff
Dawn Diggs, FDN
Maria Disciullo, BOP
Rev. L. Rita Dixon, NMD

Daily Lectionary

Ps. 5, 27, 51, 147:1-11
Jer. 18:1-11
Rom. 8:1-11; John 6:27-40

Daily Lectionary

Ps. 27, 102, 126, 147:12-20
Jer. 22:13-23
Rom. 8:12-27; John 6:41-51

RUSSIA/BELARUS/UKRAINE

"Chernobyl has been forgotten amid other world cataclysms," according to Slavomir Antonovich of the Belarussian State Committee for Chernobyl Issues. Can he be right? Have we in the Christian community in the West forgotten that horrific assault on God's creation and God's people?

International attention may have moved on, but the harsh facts remain. Sixteen years have passed since the explosion and fire at Chernobyl's No. 4 nuclear reactor near the Ukrainian-Belarussian-Russian border. In its wake, 23 percent of Belarus, 5 percent of Ukraine, and 1.5 percent of Russia lay contaminated from the radiation released in history's most devastating nuclear accident. At least 8,000 people have died, most from radiation-related diseases. About 2,000 people have been diagnosed with thyroid cancer, and as many as 10,000 more cases are expected in the next ten years.

PC(USA) church partners have not forgotten. The Round Table of Interchurch Aid in Belarus annually organizes relief for the victims of Chernobyl. Its members provide social and medical aid, rehabilitation and recreation for children, and support to families who lost their breadwinner. Orthodox, Baptist, and Lutheran brothers and sisters reach out to care for the victims. Following their example, can we do anything less than seek healing for the children of God and renewal for the creation that surrounds us daily?

RUSSIA
Total Area: 6,585,000 sq. mi. (slightly less than 1.8 times the size of the United States). **Population**: 145,470,197. **Languages**: Russian, other. **GDP Per Capita**: $7,700. **Literacy**: 98% (Male 100%, Female 97%). **Religions**: Russian Orthodox, Muslim, other. **Life Expectancy**: 67.34 years. **Human Development Index Rank**: 55.

BELARUS
Total area: 80,100 sq. mi. (slightly smaller than Kansas). **Population**: 10,350,194. **Languages**: Byelorussian, Russian, other. **GDP Per Capita**: $7,500. **Literacy**: 98% (Male 99%, Female 97%. **Religions**: Eastern Orthodox, Roman Catholic, Protestant, Jewish, Muslim. **Life Expectancy**: 68.14 years. **Human Development Index** Rank: 53.

UKRAINE
Total Area: 232,800 sq. mi. (slightly smaller than Texas). **Population**: 48,760,474. **Languages**: Ukrainian, Russian, Romanian, Polish, Hungarian. **GDP Per Capita**: $3,850. **Literacy**: 98% (Male 100%, Female 97%). **Religions**: Ukrainian Orthodox—Moscow Patriarchate, Ukrainian Orthodox—Kiev Patriarchate, Ukrainian Autocephalous Orthodox, Ukrainian Catholic (Uniate), Protestant, Jewish. **Life Expectancy**: 66.15 years. **Human Development Index** Rank: 74.

Scripture

Likewise the Spirit helps us in our weakness; for we do not know how to pray as we ought, but that very Spirit intercedes with sighs too deep for words (Rom. 8:26).

REPUBLICS OF CENTRAL ASIA

Let Us Join in Prayer for:

PC(USA) General Assembly Staff
David Dobson, PPC
Rev. Jean G. Dodds, DEDO
Stephen Dominski, BOP
Annette Donald, BOP

W"here has all the water gone?" a visitor asked when visiting the ex-seaport of Moynok along the southern shore of the Aral Sea. Located between Uzbekistan and Kazakhstan in Central Asia, the Aral Sea was once the fourth-largest inland body of water in the world. Now it is only a fraction of its original size. This is a glaring example of what can happen when it is

This weathered skeleton in what was once the thriving seaport of Moynok tells the story of the dramatic shrinking of the Aral Sea.

not recognized that the earth is the Lord's and is to be used for the welfare of all humans, now and in the future. The overproduction of cotton and other misguided practices and policies of the former Soviet Union contributed to the present state of disaster in the Aral Sea area, where there are both a high incidence of disease and 60 percent unemployment.

Responding to this situation in the province of Karakalpakstan, a Worldwide Ministries Division (WMD) partner relief and development NGO (nongovernmental organization) is relating to and working with people in the area to show the love of God through the digging of wells, water management projects, and community development efforts. A WMD worker, with help from two local residents in the former seaport, has introduced a micro-credit and small business start-up program. Expressions of encouragement and signs of hope are beginning to penetrate the mood of hopelessness in this area, which certain world organizations have researched but not assisted.

Scripture

I will raise up shepherds over them who will shepherd them, and they shall not fear any longer, or be dismayed, nor shall any be missing, says the LORD (Jer. 23:4).

Daily Lectionary
Ps. 22, 105, 130, 148
Jer. 23:1-8
Rom. 8:28-39; John 6:52-59

Let Us Join in Prayer for:

PC(USA) General Assembly Staff
Jeffery Dorris, MSS
Theodora Dorsey, BOP
Elder Eleanor Doty, DEDO

REPUBLICS OF CENTRAL ASIA,
continued

New Beginnings in Southern Tajikistan

Meanwhile, a village in southern Tajikistan, where water had not been available for ten years, now has water flowing during the two hours a day when there is electricity for the pump. Women line up at the well to fill their buckets in a region that has been drought stricken for three years. At the same time, children are expressing themselves in very basic ways with their first-ever toys of paper and crayons. Newly installed water spigots and latrines are part of a community health effort. Residents are more fully motivated to do for themselves now that they have met experienced people from the outside world demonstrating God's love for them in tangible ways. The leaders in this cluster of villages realize it is because of Jesus that they have the possibility of a new beginning in their lives and in their communities.

photo by Barbara Busse

Water is now available two hours a day in the village of these Tajik children.

Daily Lectionary

Ps. 31, 43, 143, 149
Jer. 23:9-15
Rom. 9:1-18; John 6:60-71

Scripture

Simon Peter answered [the Lord], "LORD, to whom can we go? You have the words of eternal life" (John 6:68).

THE LORD'S DAY

MINUTE FOR MISSION
PRESBYTERIAN FRONTIER FELLOWSHIP

The Nyensi driver brought his snowmobile-pulled sled, a "tundra taxi," to a stop by the settlement of six Nyensi animal-hide teepees deep in Russia's Siberian icebox. Nearby, a herd of 200 reindeer grazed the tundra. A small child (looking for all the world like a teddy bear) played in the bitterly cold snow as if it were a sandbox. Two Russian Baptist leaders and two Presbyterian Frontier Fellowship (PFF) and PC(USA) staff stepped off the sled and moved gratefully into the warmth of the teepee to learn the beliefs of the household and to tell them the story of Jesus Christ.

photo by Harold Kurtz

A Russian Baptist evangelist and Siberian guide visit a remote Siberian settlement.

Presbyterian frontier mission goes to such lengths to develop new mission partnerships—in this case with the Russian Baptist Union—that we hope and pray will spawn an indigenous following of Jesus Christ among each of the thousands of Unreached People Groups in our world today. Through our congregations, PFF, PC(USA) Worldwide Ministries, and our partner churches, Presbyterians are witnessing to Christ and planting culturally contextualized Christian churches among over 220 cultures in which the gospel has yet to take root.

Through the success of this Presbyterian outreach to the Nyensi, and similar outreach in many other cultures, we know the truth of Jesus' words, "And I, when I am lifted up from the earth, will draw all people to myself" (John 12:32).

—*Rev. David Hackett, executive director, Presbyterian Frontier Fellowship*

Prayer
Lord of the world, we pray that your story will come across clear and true through your faithful witnesses the world over. May people from the Nyensi and from every other culture call upon Christ as their Savior and give birth to strong and vital indigenous Christian movements, that your name be praised. In Jesus' name. Amen.

Sunday Lectionary and Hymns

Jer. 31:31–34
O Come Unto the Lord
PH 381

Ps. 51:1–12
Psalm 51
PH 196; PPCS 47

or Ps. 119:9–16
Blest Are the Uncorrupt in Heart
PH 233

Heb. 5:5–10
Make Me a Captive, Lord
PH 378; HB 308

John 12:20–33
Take Up Your Cross, the Savior Said
PH 393; HB 293

Daily Lectionary
Ps. 32, 42, 84, 150
Jer. 23:16-32
1 Cor. 9:19-27; Mark 8:31–9:1

Fifth Sunday in Lent • 97

Let Us Join in Prayer for:

PC(USA) People in Mission
Rev. Art Beals, regional facilitator, Albania, Kosovo, Turkey, and Azerbaijan

Partners/Ministries
Serbian Orthodox Church: **His Holiness Pavle II**, patriarch; Reformed Church in Yugoslavia: **Rev. Dr. István Csete-Szemesi**, bishop of Voivodina; Jinishian Memorial Program [Turkey]; Turkish Protestant Fellowship; **His All Holiness Bartholomew I**, ecumenical patriarch, **His Beatitude Patriarch Mesrob II of Istanbul and all Turkey**, Armenian patriarch

PC(USA) General Assembly Staff
Mary Douglass, BOP
Diana Dow, CMD

SERBIA/MONTENEGRO

As this *Mission Yearbook* is being written, the Serbian parliament has approved an accord to replace federal Yugoslavia with a new nation called Serbia and Montenegro. Before a constitution for a new state can be drafted, the parliaments of Serbia, Montenegro, and the Yugoslavian federation must ratify the accord.

Bishop Istvan Csete-Szemesi of the Reformed Christian Church in Yugoslavia wrote to the Presbyterian Church (U.S.A.) after the attacks of September 11, 2001, to express the church's solidarity. "We were one with you, with the members of PC(USA), and with all citizens of your country, asking the Lord to keep and preserve you from evil forces. We bring you before the Lord in our prayers all the time since that incomparably tragic event. But we trust nothing can separate us from each other, neither life, nor death, as we are one in the love of Christ."

He wrote that after the end of communist rule in 2002, some church buildings were in ruins. Small congregations saw a pastor only occasionally. He explained the desire of the church to form centers for these scattered, small congregations.

Total Area: 39,400 sq. mi. (slightly smaller than Kentucky). **Population**: 10,677,290. **Languages**: Serbian, Albanian. **GDP Per Capita**: $2,300. **Literacy**: 93% (Male 97.2%, Female 88.9%). **Religions**: Orthodox, Muslim, Roman Catholic, Protestant, other. **Life Expectancy**: 73.5 years. **Human Development Index Rank**: NA.

TURKEY

Presbyterians are able to reach out to the people of Turkey through Extra Commitment Opportunities (ECO). Funds are provided for children and youth ministries as young people respond to the gospel through newly established Turkish Protestant churches. Several camps and conference programs are designed to meet the needs of those whose families have limited financial means. Another ECO program provides emergency health care. Through the Istanbul Mercy Ministry and Church Growth Fund, the Besiktas Turkish Protestant Church of Istanbul offers food and shelter to street children, housing and job training for widows and single mothers, and aid to earthquake refugee communities.

Total Area: 297,200 sq. mi. (slightly larger than Texas). **Population**: 66,493,970. **Languages**: Turkish (official), Kurdish, Arabic, Armenian, Greek. **GDP Per Capita**: $6,800. **Literacy**: 85%. **Religions**: Muslim, other. **Life Expectancy**: 71.24 years. **Human Development Index Rank**: 82.

Daily Lectionary

Ps. 6, 119:73-80, 121, 145
Jer. 24:1-10
Rom. 9:19-33; John 9:1-17

Scripture
I will give them a heart to know that I am the LORD; and they shall be my people and I will be their God, for they shall return to me with their whole heart (Jer. 24:7).

SWITZERLAND

Initiated by the Presbyterian Church some forty years ago under the leadership of Margaret Flory, Frontier Internship in Mission (FIM) supports a program of three-year internships in all regions of the world. With the full cooperation of the PC(USA), FIM has become an international ecumenical program, supported by some twenty national churches and agencies in North America, Europe, and Asia. FIM is based at the Ecumenical Center in Geneva, Switzerland. Recent Frontiers have included the clearing of land mines in Cambodia; the support of churches engaged in land rights issues in Chiapas, Guatemala, Honduras, and Botswana; work with national churches in Africa on HIV/AIDS policy; the development of Internet capacities with ecumenical groups in Palestine; literacy work and training in conflict resolution in Lebanon, Jordan, Morocco, and Egypt; peace building in Kosovo; and the support of churches working for the unification of North and South Korea. Frontier Interns are engaged in communities of faith committed to justice. With their church and ecumenical organizations they build common strategies to confront injustice in a global context. In recent years interns have met for orientation, global analysis, and training in Bangkok, Quito, Nanjing, and Yaoundé. The overall work of FIM is directed by an International Coordinating Committee representing churches, ecumenical bodies, and the World Student Christian Federation in all regions of the world.

The International Coordinating Committee met in Havana, Cuba.

Total Area: 15,300 sq. mi. (slightly less than twice the size of New Jersey). **Population**: 7,283,274. **Languages**: German (official), French (official), Italian (official), Romansch, other. **GDP Per Capita**: $28,600. **Literacy**: 99%. **Religions**: Roman Catholic, Protestant, other, none. **Life Expectancy**: 79.73 years. **Human Development Index Rank**: 11.

Scripture

"One thing I do know, that though I was blind, now I see" (John 9:25).

Let Us Join in Prayer for:

PC(USA) People in Mission
Rev. John Roaldseth Moyer, director, Frontier Intern in Mission Program

Partners/Ministries
John Knox International Reformed Center; World Alliance of Reformed Churches: **Rev. Setri Nyomi**, general secretary; Federation of Swiss Protestant Churches: **Rev. Thomas Wipf**, president; World Council of Churches: **Rev. Dr. Konrad Raiser**, general secretary; Bossey Ecumenical Institute; Conference of European Churches: **Rev. Dr. Keith Clements**, general secretary

PC(USA) General Assembly Staff
Scott Dowd, CMD
Lori Dowell, PPC

Daily Lectionary

Ps. 25, 34, 91, 146
Jer. 25:8-17
Rom. 10:1-13; John 9:18-41

THE SYNOD OF LINCOLN TRAILS

Let Us Join in Prayer for:

Synod Staff
Rev. James L. Hudson, co-executive
Rev. Carol M. McDonald, co-executive
Rev. David D. Crittenden, co-executive
Suellen Burnett, administrative assistant
Kristi Miller, administrative assistant
Judith Wolfred, administrative assistant

PC(USA) General Assembly Staff
Thomas Dragani, BOP
Edward Driscoll, BOP
Diane Dulaney, MSS

The Synod of Lincoln Trails and its congregations and presbyteries wish to be a partner with God in restoring right relationship with the earth and its inhabitants. To that end the Synod of Lincoln Trails uses some of the mission dollars entrusted to it for two grant programs available to Presbyterians in Indiana and Illinois. The Biblical Literacy grant is for congregations that want to design and implement programming that focuses on teaching the Bible and increasing biblical literacy among their members. The Prophetic Action grant is for church sessions, clusters of several congregations, presbytery councils, and presbytery social justice committees. This grant encourages the planning of programs and events that focus on discerning the challenges to God's people in carrying out the will of God. Previously, program designs included protecting and restoring natural resources, reducing violence in society, and furthering economic and racial justice.

In 2001 a Prophetic Action grant was given to Wabash Avenue Presbyterian Church in Crawfordsville, Indiana. The grant sponsored a Gifts for Guns program. During the month of December persons in this rural community who wanted to dispose of firearms could exchange them for $50 in cash to spend on Christmas gifts for their loved ones. The congregational members who came up with the idea and implemented it were motivated by their belief that gun-related violence is not confined to inner cities but happens in all communities. Fifty-one unwanted guns were received, and forty-seven were exchanged for $50 each. The congregation plans to make Gifts for Guns an annual event.

The 692 churches in the Synod of Lincoln Trails have 154,813 members. McCormick Theological Seminary in Chicago is within synod bounds.

Daily Lectionary

Ps. 5, 27, 51, 147:1-11
Jer. 25:30-38
Rom. 10:14-21; John 10:1-18

Scripture

"I have other sheep that do not belong to this fold. I must bring them also, and they will listen to my voice. So there will be one flock, one shepherd" (John 10:16).

THE PRESBYTERY OF BLACKHAWK

Illinois

Members of Westminster Presbyterian Church in DeKalb have created an innovative evangelism and discipleship outreach for college students. In 1994 the congregation designed a parish-based campus ministry that nurtured relationships between the families of the rural, university community and college students, many of whom were from the Chicago area. With the collaborative efforts of a newly hired associate pastor, DeKalb residents invited these young adults from Northern Illinois University and Kishwaukee College to their homes on a monthly basis for meals. Members of the church encouraged the college students' involvement in the life of the church through a warm welcome to join Sunday worship services, participate as liturgists, and share in Sunday Bible studies. The students created a bimonthly, midweek Taizé service that continued for several years. Church families shared in ministry outreach with collegians through projects such as Habitat for Humanity. They assisted in staffing The Listening Post, a place on each campus where any passerby is offered an understanding ear. The Session supported the inclusion of various lecturers and speakers from such places of higher learning as McCormick Seminary, the University of Chicago, and Wheaton College. Church leaders designed the award-winning Last Lecture series, premised on what a professor would offer as a final lecture. Westminster members delivered care packages during final exams for these newest members of their church community.

Participants strive to fulfill their mission statement, which reads, "a group for all seeking a community of warm friendship, searching questions, and faith in action."

As this ministry grows in the new millennium, the church shapes its outreach to address the current needs of the students. According to the associate pastor, the Rev. Karen Herbst Kim, the college group meets twice weekly. On Sunday mornings there is in-depth discussion about a challenging faith issue. Tuesday evenings are a time of fellowship and prayer. Service projects remain a cohesive component of the ministry. Participants in the ministry strive to fulfill their mission statement, which reads, "a group on and off campus for all seeking a community of warm friendship, searching questions, and faith in action."

Presbytery of Blackhawk has 1 new church development and 88 churches with 18,785 members.

Scripture

The LORD has done great things for us, and we rejoiced (Ps. 126:3).

Let Us Join in Prayer for:

Elder Dorothy J. Henderson, member, GAC

Presbytery Staff
Rev. Dr. John E. Rickard, general presbyter
Rev. John C. Huff, stated clerk/treasurer
Rev. William Lawser, congregational development specialist
Joy Butler, resource center coordinator
Gary L. Batty, executive director, Stronghold Camp and Conference Center
Barbara Kirchner, administrative assistant

PC(USA) General Assembly Staff
Richard Dunaway, DEDO
Catherine Duncan, CMD
Sharon Dunne, PW

Daily Lectionary

Ps. 27, 102, 126, 147:12-20
Jer. 26:1-16 (17-24); Rom. 11:1-12
John 10:19-42

Let Us Join in Prayer for:

Elder E. Dolores Register, member, GAC

Presbytery Staff
Elder Rose Blaney, coord. of scholarship funds; **Deacon Betsy Cairns**, receptionist; **Rev. Carlos Correa**, exec. director, Urban Youth Ministry; **Elder Marcia Escudero**, social justice ministries coord.; **Omar Garlaza**, program director, Urban Youth Ministry; **Edith Hill**, admin. asst., camps and conferences ministries; **Rev. Joseph Hill**, director, camps and conferences ministries; **Elder Carlene Hyrams**, associate exec.; **Kieth Kliver**, accounting manager; **Rev. Kathryn Ksander**, recording clerk; **Elder Lessie Mallory**, Committee on Ministry (COM) regional coord.; **Elder Robert McBride**, COM regional coord.; **Agnes Murphy**, admin. asst.; **Elder Carole Norton**, COM regional coord./Committee on Preparation for Ministry coord.; **Earnestine Norwood**, office manager; **Elder Grace Ohman**, receptionist; **Brenda Pious**, staff accountant; **Dave Rastall**, caretaker, camps and conferences ministries; **Rev. Robert Reynolds**, exec. presbyter; **Elder Tamika Stewart**, accounting asst.; **Elder Herbert A. Smyers**, director, business affairs; **Glen Wagner**, mailroom clerk/groundskeeper; **Elder Janet Wilson**, associate exec. and stated clerk; **Mary Hartmann**, **Elder Betty McGinnis**, **Kitty Ridley**, and **Elder Allena Williams**, exec. assistants

PC(USA) General Assembly Staff
Rev. Dr. Miriam Dunson, CMD

Daily Lectionary

Ps. 22, 105, 130, 148; Jer. 29:1 (2-3) 4-14
Rom 11:13-24
John 11:1-27 or John 12:1-10

THE PRESBYTERY OF CHICAGO

Illinois

The Presbytery of Chicago is where God is gathering a welcoming, worshiping, and witnessing Christian Community." This, the presbytery's vision statement, recognizes that "the earth is the LORD's and all . . . those who live in it." It is God's activity that empowers the presbytery's churches and members to "bring people together in mission" and "live at peace with each other."

Worship at Pullman Presbyterian Church in Chicago is enriched by the partnership with First Presbyterian Church of Glen Ellyn.

One expression of this commitment is the partnership between First Presbyterian Church in Glen Ellyn and Pullman Presbyterian Church in Chicago. This urban/suburban, cross-cultural partnership has brought two diverse congregations together for worship, prayer breakfasts, Presbyterian Women's meetings, mission fairs, and mission service projects.

One Sunday the two churches held a joint worship service, using the chapel at Wheaton College to accommodate both congregations. The pastors—the Rev. Jerry Andrews of Glen Ellyn First and the Rev. Eddie Knox of Chicago Pullman—and the choirs of both churches participated. Worship was followed by a time of fellowship.

Pullman participated in Glen Ellyn's mission fair as one of its mission partners. The men's groups from the two churches worked together as a mission team at First Presbyterian in Chicago, doing needed painting. The two churches also share concerns for many social justice issues, such as crime, drugs, and alcohol abuse.

Both churches are involved in capital campaigns that include building expansions and are part of the presbytery's Building Partnerships Campaign. The presbytery's campaign is focused on five cornerstone churches, including Pullman, whose financial needs exceed their resources. Glen Ellyn participates in the presbytery's campaign and has directed $100,000 to Pullman's ministry as a mission component of its own campaign, "Building Tomorrow's Ministry Today." The partnerships include much more than financial support, as the Glen Ellyn-Pullman partnership illustrates.

The Presbytery of Chicago includes 108 churches with 40,862 members.

Scripture

For surely I know the plans I have for you, says the Lord, plans for your welfare and not for harm, to give you a future with hope (Jer. 29:11).

THE PRESBYTERY OF GREAT RIVERS

Illinois

The partnership between the Presbytery of Great Rivers and the Presbytery of Northeast Brazil has blessed both groups of people, giving them a chance to feel the presence of the Holy Spirit moving in their midst. Since 1999 Great Rivers has sent four work/study teams representing twenty-three churches to Brazil. It is currently working with the Presbytery of Northeast Brazil in Pendencias, Alto do Rodrigues, Macau, and Mossoro on projects that include starting microenterprises and building multifunctional church buildings that provide jobs, job training, and day-care programs. One work team held a hygiene clinic at the church in Mossoro to which it brought toothpaste, toothbrushes, mouthwash, soap, shampoo, and other items. Expecting 60 children, the group had 120 eager children to teach. Groups from the Presbytery of Northeast Brazil have also visited the Presbytery of Great Rivers, the latest being a delegation from the Assu Valley that visited in November 2002. Abigail Noadia Barthaldo da Silva, a professor from the Center for Missionary Training in Natal, Brazil, has been part of the exchange between the two presbyteries. She graduated in June 2002 from McCormick Theological Seminary, where she received a master's degree in mission.

Great Rivers has also been involved at home. During 2002 the presbytery supported domestic violence shelters and drop-in centers within its boundaries as a special mission project. The presbytery's Matching Grant program provided funds for agencies ranging from infant care centers, crisis centers, domestic violence centers, after-school programs, day camps, homeless shelters, and breadlines.

The Presbytery of Great Rivers has 118 churches with 22,783 members. Three Presbyterian colleges are within its bounds: Blackburn College in Carlinville, Illinois College in Jacksonville, and Monmouth College in Monmouth.

Children attend a hygiene clinic held at a church in Mossoro, Brazil.

Scripture

O the depth of the riches and wisdom and knowledge of God! How unsearchable are [God's] judgments and how inscrutable [are God's] ways! . . . For from [God] and through [God] and to [God] are all things. To [God] be the glory forever. Amen (Rom. 11:33–36).

Let Us Join in Prayer for:

Presbytery Staff
Paul Gregory Neel, interim executive presbyter/stated clerk
Sherry Stottler, associate executive presbyter
Bradley C. Clark, associate executive presbyter
Etta M. Park, business manager
Barbara L. Hartwig, administrative assistant
Diane Lovell, receptionist/clerk

PC(USA) General Assembly Staff
Elder Bettie Durrah, NMD
Amelia Dye, BOP
Cindy Ealy, OGA
Rev. Stephen Earl, WMD

Daily Lectionary

Ps. 31, 43, 143, 149; Jer. 31:27-34
Rom. 11:25-36; John 11:28-44
or John 12:37-50

Sunday Lectionary and Hymns

Mark 11:1–11
Ride On! Ride On in Majesty!
PH 90/91; HB 188

or John 12:12–16
Ride On! Ride On in Majesty!
PH 90/91; HB 188

Ps. 118:1–2, 19–29
By Gracious Powers
PH 342; PPCS 118

Isa. 50:4–9a
When Morning Lights the Eastern Skies
PH 250; HB 49

Ps. 31:9–16
Psalm 31:9–16
PH 182

Phil. 2:5–11
At the Name of Jesus
PH 148; HB 143

Mark 14:1–15:47
or Mark 15:1–39 (40–47)
O Sacred Head, Now Wounded
PH 98; HB 194

Daily Lectionary
Ps. 32, 42, 84, 150; Zech. 9:9-12
or Zech. 12:9-11, 13:1, 7-9
1 Tim. 6:12-16; Matt. 21:12-17

THE LORD'S DAY

MINUTE FOR MISSION
PASSION/PALM SUNDAY

"I am the scorn of all my adversaries, a horror to my neighbors, an object of dread to my acquaintances; those who see me in the street flee from me" (Ps. 31:11).

Ruth Mae Harris lives in a group home for developmentally disabled adults. She has that "horror to my neighbors" look about her. Plenty of folks cross the street when they see her approaching.

Ruth Mae came to church on the Sunday that the confirmands marched forward to profess faith. One of the kids was going to be baptized. Ruth Mae stood up from her pew and walked slowly to the front of the sanctuary. The congregation's anxiety grew—"Who is that?" "What does she want?"

Ruth Mae wanted to be saved, she said. "Let your face shine upon your servant; save me in your steadfast love" (Ps. 31:16). So I invited her to the font. "Do you believe in Jesus?" I asked. "Yes, I do," she proclaimed. I placed wet fingers on her head. "I baptize you in the name of the Father, the Son, and the Holy Spirit." Ruth Mae returned to her pew.

I learned a long time ago that decent and orderly worship and well-planned meetings honor God. Time and again, however, grace has emerged in the most surprising ways—when a well-planned event gives birth to something unforeseen. If I had been in charge, the Palm Sunday parade would have included only the well-scrubbed. People like Ruth Mae help me remember that regardless of my plans, God's invitation refuses to be controlled. The procession to the cross includes misfits—which is to say, all of us—whose profession is not always well rehearsed, who don't always behave faithfully or politely, yet who seek God's salvation in the only ways they can. In that, God is glorified.

Ruth Mae came to worship the next week. She was a bit upset. "All the others got a gift," she said. "Do I get one?" She meant the confirmands, but in my mind, the whole church received a gift that day. "Yes, Ruth Mae. There's a gift for you."

—*Rev. Mark D. Hinds, former associate editor, curriculum development, Congregational Ministries Publishing*

Prayer
O Christ, you choose paths that cross boundaries and bid us follow. May our feet not stumble as we seek to go where you lead. In your name. Amen.

MIDWEST HANMI PRESBYTERY

Nongeographic

Many churches of Midwest Hanmi Presbytery send out short-term mission teams, and groups have gone to countries in Africa, Asia, the Middle East, and South America, and to Russia and the republics of Central Asia.

Moved by Jesus' ministries outlined in Matt. 4:23-24 and the Great Commission, the college student group of Fullness Presbyterian Church in Chicago

College students from Fullness Presbyterian Church play with the children of Meru, Kenya.

made a mission trip for a month to the village of Meru, Kenya. After two years of planning, fund-raising, information gathering, and collecting pharmaceuticals, school supplies, and food stuff, the church sent seven young adults and the Rev. Ji Suk Kim. Arriving in Nairobi, Kenya, they traveled by car for three hours and on foot for an hour to a small village where there was no electricity. A Korean mission worker stationed in Kenya for twenty years guided the team, and an African pastor named Amon assisted them with translation.

The mission team was divided into three work teams. One team taught children English, math, and science; another taught Bible; and the third team instructed them in gospel music, dance, and crafts. In the afternoons the mission workers played folk games, danced, or sang with village people; worked on a church building project; instructed villagers about wellness and hygiene; visited sick people in their homes; and told people on the streets about the gospel. On Sundays the college students and villagers held worship services together.

Those things that the college students of Fullness Presbyterian most valued during their trip were sharing meals with brothers and sisters in a remote African village, the challenging plunge into a variety of African cultures, the value of togetherness, and their meager efforts to improve the quality of life of shoeless children in Meru, Kenya.

The nongeographical Presbytery of Midwest Hanmi has 26 member churches, including 5 new church developments, and 3,759 members.

Scripture

Forgetting what lies behind and straining forward to what lies ahead, I press on toward the goal for the prize of the heavenly call of God in Christ Jesus (Phil. 3:13–14).

Let Us Join in Prayer for:

Presbytery Staff
Rev. Harold Shin, executive presbyter
Rev. Se-Bong Kan, stated clerk

PC(USA) General Assembly Staff
Melinda Ebbs, DEDO
Celeste Eck, BOP
Anna Edlin, FDN

Daily Lectionary
Ps. 6, 119:73-80, 121, 145
Jer. 11:18-20, 12:1-16 (17)
Phil. 3:1-14; John 12:9-19

THE PRESBYTERY OF OHIO VALLEY

Indiana

Let Us Join in Prayer for:

Presbytery Staff
Rev. Lorna Kuyk, executive presbyter
Rev. Fred Page, stated clerk, associate executive presbyter
Rev. John McKune, treasurer
Gayle Burns, administrative assistant, resource center coordinator

PC(USA) General Assembly Staff
Elder Joe Edmiston, MSS
Laura Edwards, FDN
Stephanie Egnotovich, PPC

The mission of the Presbytery of Ohio Valley, composed of small to midsized churches, is to serve its congregations as they fulfill their call. One of its smallest churches, First Presbyterian Church of Paoli, Indiana, experienced a crisis when fire completely destroyed its historic building just before Christmas in 2000. The congregation quickly learned it was not alone. The denomination provided a Disaster Assistance grant, and the presbytery provided a commission to assist this congregation facing many challenges. Support came from other churches in the form of prayer, financial assistance, donations of hymnals, and even a communion service (for 500!). The 2001 General Assembly's worship service held in Louisville, Kentucky, included the Paoli church in its offering.

First Presbyterian Church in Paoli, Indiana, received support from the whole Presbyterian Church (U.S.A.).

Members of the congregation and the commission began a journey of faith to assess the church's mission in the community. A mission study took place over thirteen weeks that emphasized prayer and fellowship. The members came to know one another as a family of God while naming their needs and assessing the needs of the community. The mission study provided new identity for members as followers of Jesus Christ through worship, prayer, Christian witness, and compassionate outreach.

With this re-formed sense of identity came a building that now serves the needs of the church and the community. The new building reflects the history and tradition of the church and represents a transformed congregation that is clear about its vision and mission.

Support from the PC(USA) was instrumental in renewing the spirit of the church as a part of the body of Christ, and the Paoli church rejoices in the ways that the presbytery has strengthened the church in fulfilling its mission.

The Presbytery of Ohio Valley has 85 churches with 9,591 members.

Daily Lectionary
Ps. 25, 34, 91, 146
Jer. 15:10-21
Phil. 3:15-2; John 12:20-26

Scripture
"Sir, we wish to see Jesus" (John 12:21).

THE PRESBYTERY OF SOUTHEASTERN ILLINOIS

Here we are, living with the steadily increasing desire for things to be different. Here we are, often dragging our cross in fear, fear that makes us reluctant to take up the cross, to trust in Christ's promise that "my burden is light," readily bearable. Here we are, tempted to believe that what God is glad to give us might not be enough.

Yet here we are, responding to Christ's call to lead, to proclaim the good news that God is with us, that God loves us, and that in God's love, we become new persons.

Here we are, purposefully moving along in response to this good news, committed to growing in our knowing and to acting with integrity in our doing.

Here we are, remembering that our growing in faith depends on our commitment to disciplines and practices that bind us together and keep us committed to this journey, in community, following Christ Jesus.

Here we are, responding in hope to Jesus' invitation to keep moving into deeper and deeper relationship with each other and God, on the wonderful, challenging journey in which hope increases, peace emerges, and joy abounds.

We in the Presbytery of Southeastern Illinois are convinced that leadership development is the most important and urgent developmental need for the church and therefore the most important issue for congregations. We struggle faithfully to discover and develop appropriate ways to encourage, nurture, and support our current clergy and lay leaders who work with the presbytery's 103 churches with 13,248 members. Millikin University in Decatur is within the bounds of the presbytery.

> *We . . . are convinced that leadership development is the most important and urgent developmental need for the church and therefore the most important issue for congregations.*

Let Us Join in Prayer for:

Presbytery Staff
Elder Richard C. Malmberg, executive presbyter
Elder Marie V. McNabb, stated clerk
Rev. Richard L. Ryman, Camp Carew director
Elder David H. Marshall, treasurer
Rev. William Lawser, congregational development specialist
Rev. David MacDonna, executive presbyter emeritus
Brenda Harvey, administrative assistant
Marti Bartels, secretary

PC(USA) General Assembly Staff
Elder Vanessa Elkin, FDN
Elder Jean C. Elliott, DEDO

Scripture

Heal me, O LORD, and I shall be healed; save me, and I shall be saved; for you are my praise (Jer. 17:14).

Daily Lectionary
Ps. 5, 27, 51, 147:1-11
Jer. 17:5-10, 14-17 (18)
Phil. 4:1-13; John 12:27-36

Wednesday of Holy Week • 107

Let Us Join in Prayer for:

PC(USA) General Assembly Staff
Shari Elliott, PPC
Cornelia Ellis, CMD
Jennifer Ellis, PPC

MAUNDY THURSDAY

MINUTE FOR MISSION

As I write for the *Mission Yearbook*, family members of four very dear friends are having tests done to find answers to questions they wish they'd never have to ask: Has the cancer spread? Did the surgery and the first round of chemo get it all? Does Dad have symptoms of Parkinson's? What is your best guess on how long Mom has to live?

Reading from the John 13 passage, it appears that the disciples had their own questions as Jesus broke bread with them and washed their feet: Who is this man? Is he "King of Israel" or a servant who washes feet? Where is he going? Why can't I follow him?

Maundy Thursday is a somber occasion in the life of the church. We know that on that evening, Jesus was betrayed by one friend and denied by another, and he was crucified the next day. The Scripture tells us that the disciples did not understand. Over two thousand years later, we have a better vantage point than they did. We know the joy of Easter morning—but not just yet.

God's grace abounds through the love that Jesus showed to his disciples when he washed their feet. That grace and love continue through the care and affection we show to one another in Christ's name.

As I write, the sun is shining brightly, but clouds loom in my heart. I tell myself, it's okay to feel somber and sad. It's okay to question what tomorrow may bring and how those I love will cope if the news is not good. It's okay not to understand it all. It's okay because it isn't the last word and we are not alone. God's grace abounds through the love that Jesus showed to his disciples when he washed their feet. That grace and love continue through the care and affection we show to one another in Christ's name. And, most of all, Easter morning is just around the corner.

—*Elder Dr. Beth Basham, associate manager,
planning/project management, General Assembly Council*

Daily Lectionary
Ps. 27, 102, 126, 147:12-20
Jer. 20:7-11 (12-13) 14-18
1 Cor. 10:14-17, 11:27-32
John 17:1-11 (12-26)

Prayer
Creator of all: For welcoming our questions and loving us on somber days, we give you thanks. For resurrection joy that embraces us in moments of sadness as we face our deepest doubts and concerns, we praise your holy name. Help us to know best how to share Christ's servant love to one another. In Jesus' name. Amen.

GOOD FRIDAY

MINUTE FOR MISSION

Good Friday. The name seems like such a misnomer. What's good about the harsh reality that confronts us on this day? What's good about the betrayal and fickleness reflected in the notable activities of this day? What's good about remembering such bleakness and woe? If we didn't have the privilege of knowing the whole story, of seeing beyond the moment, of appreciating the outcome, it would be difficult to observe Good Friday, but thankfully we have that unique perspective. Good Friday gives us an indelible image of goodness, an image based on a sacrifice that marks a beginning instead of punctuating an end, the beginning of a new, indestructible hope and a fresh understanding of a very old love.

In Heb. 10:23, we are urged to "hold fast to the confession of our hope without wavering, for [God] who has promised is faithful." In addition, we are asked to "consider how to provoke one another to love and good deeds" (vs. 24). Clearly, this indelible image of goodness helps spur us on to ministries of love.

> *Jesus' sacrifice creates for us an indelible image of goodness. Mission provides a way for us to emulate and exhibit that image.*

The National Ministries Division of the Presbyterian Church (U.S.A.) traditionally sponsors a Mission USA Tour for the moderator of the General Assembly. The tour serves a dual purpose. It helps to showcase some of the outstanding work in mission being done by Presbyterians across the nation, and it gives the denomination a chance to express its sincere appreciation to those on the front lines of mission. And make no mistake about it: Presbyterians do an exceptional job in mission all over the world. Despite well-publicized disputes of recent times, there is more than ample evidence that Presbyterians continue to spur one another on toward love and good deeds. Jesus' sacrifice creates for us an indelible image of goodness. Mission provides a way for us to emulate and exhibit that image.

—Rev. Curtis A. Kearns, Jr., director, National Ministries Division

Prayer

Gracious and powerful God, we thank you for your sacrifice in Jesus and for the indelible image of goodness and love it creates for us. Help us to see beyond the prevalence of bleakness and woe to the hope of Christ's victory, and help us to be instruments of that goodness. In Jesus' name. Amen.

Let Us Join in Prayer for:

PC(USA) General Assembly Staff
Elder Robert Ellis, FDN
Rev. Robert Ellis, WMD
Cynthia Embry, MSS

Daily Lectionary

Ps. 22, 105, 130, 148
Gen. 22:1-14; 1 Peter 1:10-20
John 13:36-38 or John 19:38-42

Let Us Join in Prayer for:

Elder Gregg Neel, member, GAC
Rev. Nancy Kahaian, member, GAC

Presbytery Staff
Rev. Sue Berry, general presbyter
Elder Paul D. Fogg, associate presbyter
for Geneva Center
Rev. David Smook, pastor to pastors
Elder James Emerson, stated clerk
Gladys Sargent, office manager
Elder Cathy Hahn, recording clerk
Elder Harold L. Gray, treasurer
Pauline Donaldson, bookkeeper
Shelly Gibson, receptionist, secretary

PC(USA) General Assembly Staff
Bertram Emeka-Ekwue, WMD
Darolyn Emerson, MSS
Derek Emerson, DEDO

THE PRESBYTERY OF WABASH VALLEY *Indiana*

Harry Hoover, a member of Earl Park Presbyterian Church, and Rossville Presbyterian Church youth help a pastor of Ciudad Juarez build a home.

The Presbytery of Wabash Valley celebrates its mission in word and deed, offering support and resources for 99 congregations with 21,085 members. New connections are emerging as creative ways to work effectively. The Mission Action and Interpretation Committee has joined with the staff of Geneva Center, the presbytery's camp and conference center, to organize more traveling opportunities for serving Christ in the world. These two groups bring together the vision and the skills for year-round planning and leading into places of need.

Mission giving and involvement go hand-in-hand in congregations as they respond to the gospel of Jesus Christ. The First Presbyterian Church of Frankfort is committed to growing in both areas. Its hope is to visit each of the mission interests it supports in the course of five years with teams of two or three people. The focus will be pastoral in nature as the groups encourage and care for the mission workers, learn about their ministry, and then communicate the vitality of their experience to members back home.

Many churches send groups to work on short-term projects. For the last ten years, a cluster of congregations has been active in global service and education by partnering to travel and work, most recently in Ciudad Juarez, Mexico, where they built a school. The cooperative effort of the churches makes the project financially possible for every church participating.

Closer to home, the people of Westminster Presbyterian Church in Munster use a model of local mission called "Take It to Town!" From Second Presbyterian Church in Indianapolis they learned about this annual, day-long involvement of more than one hundred members in hands-on ministry in nearby communities. Projects for the day included cleaning up the Lake Michigan shoreline, serving meals at the Hammond Warming Shelter, working on Teen Center rooms at First Presbyterian Church in Gary, participating in Adopt a Block repairs and cleanup, and visiting with residents of Hartsfield Village, an asssisted-living facility.

Daily Lectionary

Ps. 31, 43, 143, 149; Job 19:21-27a
Heb. 4:1-16; Rom. 8:1-11

Scripture

For I know that my Redeemer lives, and that at the last [the Lord] will stand upon the earth (Job 19:25).

THE LORD'S DAY

MINUTE FOR MISSION
ONE GREAT HOUR OF SHARING/EASTER

Today we celebrate a triumph without parallel in history, the triumph of life over death, of grace over law, of love over hostility and alienation. We celebrate God's Son's willing self-sacrifice for our sake, and the transformative power of that sacrifice. Truly, it is a moment of profound joy.

Jesus' sacrifice is a model, an invitation, and a challenge. The one who gave himself for our sins is also the one who told us to pick up our cross and follow him, who reminded us that in order to save our lives we would have to lose them. Those words may have sounded noble to his disciples before the crucifixion, but they must have had an awful edge that terrible Friday night and on Saturday, as the reality sank in. Yet Easter proclaims anew this challenge that is also a promise: giving oneself to others is paradoxically the only way to a life that transcends death.

The theme for this year's One Great Hour of Sharing comes from 1 Peter. "Like stewards of the manifold grace of God, serve one another with whatever gift each of you has received." It speaks to the gifts that are particular to each of us—a musical talent, an ability to organize details, an intuitive understanding of others. We bring these gifts to whatever we do, and they enrich our abilities to share with others. But as Christians, we have all been given the ultimate gift, the gift that frees us from the narrow bounds of our own limitations and failings. That gift of God's love in Jesus blesses us not when we try to grasp it, but when we pass it on to others.

Through One Great Hour of Sharing, Presbyterians have an opportunity to pass on that blessing, to give sacrificially for others. Some people's need is urgent, such as those facing a disaster, while others face an accumulation of chronic need—the time it takes to walk three miles carrying water, the lack of education and health care. Our gifts to One Great Hour of Sharing witness to people in all these circumstances, proclaiming God's love in the most tangible of ways. Today, may our gifts to One Great Hour of Sharing make that proclamation resound throughout the world.

—Elder Alan B. Krome, associate, Mission Interpretation and Promotion

Prayer

Risen Lord, While the pain of your wounds and death is still raw upon our hearts, the gaping tomb proclaims that even death cannot contain the power of your love. Rather than denying the suffering of the world, your resurrection shows us that in taking that suffering as our own, we can help open it to the transforming power of your love. Help us trust in your grace to sustain us, allow your Spirit to guide our steps, and offer our hands to the service of those in need. As this day offers us new life, may our gifts today to One Great Hour of Sharing be a new beginning for our efforts to follow in the path of love you have shown us. In your name we pray. Amen.

Sunday Lectionary and Hymns

Acts 10:34–43
I Danced in the Morning
PH 302

or Isa. 25:6–9
Christ Is Risen
PH 109

Psalm 118: 1–2, 14–24
Psalm 118:14–24
PH 231; PPCS 119, 120

1 Cor. 15:1–11
Christ Is Risen! Shout Hosanna!
PH 104

or Acts 10:34–43
I Danced in the Morning
PH 302

John 20:1–18
Christ the Lord Is Risen Today!
PH 113

or Mark 16:1–8
Celebrate with Joy and Singing
PH 107

Daily Lectionary

Ps. 93, 117, 136, 150; Exod. 12:1–14
John 1:1–18 or Isa. 51:9–11
Luke 24:13–35 or John 20:19–23

Let Us Join in Prayer for:

Elder Katherine Hirt Eggleston, member, GAC

Presbytery Staff
Rev. Jill M. Hudson, co-executive presbyter/HOS
Rev. Dr. W. Keith Geckeler, co-executive presbyter/SC
Rev. Amy Williams Fowler, associate executive presbyter, congregational development and service teams
Rev. Eric Lohe, new church development pastor
Rev. James Noble, new church development pastor
Richard Swartwood, executive director, Camp PYOCA
Leah Webb, program director, Camp PYOCA
Kristy Quinn, administrative assistant, office management
Jennifer Turman, administrative assistant, finances
Erin Rhodes, administrative assistant and information technology coordinator
Ruth Ann MacPherson, receptionist and general office assistant
Ken Hall, assistant treasurer
Fabio Socarraz, community worker with the Hispanic community

PC(USA) General Assembly Staff
Charles Engleman, MSS
Rev. John Evans, FDN

Daily Lectionary

Ps. 97, 115, 124, 145
Jon. 2:1-10
Acts 2:14, 22-32; John 14:1-14

THE PRESBYTERY OF WHITEWATER VALLEY *Indiana*

Churches of the Presbytery of Whitewater Valley reflect God's love in their care for others through mission. Orchard Park Presbyterian and Westminster Presbyterian in Indianapolis and First Presbyterian of Greenfield are examples of this love.

Members of Westminster Presbyterian Church in Indianapolis prepare gifts for neighborhood families.

Begun in an apple orchard forty-five years ago, Orchard Park Presbyterian has just doubled the size of its facilities. It added a large multipurpose room with showers to host Interfaith Hospitality Network guests (homeless families eager to return to normal lives); space for an English as a Second Language program for the Hispanic families whose children attend the nearby elementary school; additional classrooms for the Learning Center Christian Preschool; and a family life area for a growing youth ministry. The church also has its hands in international mission as its associate pastor, the Rev. Mike Ireland, coordinates the International Partnership with the Presbytery of Northern Quintana Roo in Mexico. Twenty Whitewater Valley congregations are helping this presbytery start eleven new churches in the next five years.

First Presbyterian Church of Greenfield engages in three mission fund-raisers. Liz'buth Anne's Kitchen serves the James Whitcomb Riley Festival by having the church's youth take orders from exhibitors and then deliver meals prepared by the women's group. Once a month in the winter the men host a chili lunch and supper with proceeds earmarked for local mission. A strawberry festival brings members across generations together.

Westminster Presbyterian Church has fewer than 60 members, yet, by partnering with several other Presbyterian churches, it provides food, clothing, and presents to over 120 neighborhood families each Christmas. These same partners help with rehabilitating nearby homes, a major tutoring and job preparedness program for youth, and a food program that feeds about 50 families a week.

Whitewater Valley is a presbytery of 69 churches, 2 new church developments, and 24,700 members.

Scripture

"In my Father's house there are many dwelling places. If it were not so, would I have told you that I go to prepare a place for you?" (John 14:2).

Earth Day

THE SYNOD OF LIVING WATERS

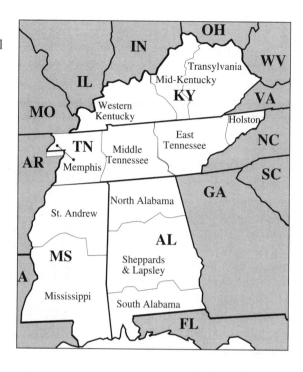

Working outside the geographical bounds of the Synod of Living Waters, members and friends of the synod's Living Waters for the World committee are helping to provide clean drinking water in such locations as Haiti, Honduras, and Mexico to people who suffer from the deadly effects of pollutants in the water they have to drink. The work of this committee grew out of the Synod Hunger Network in 1992, with the belief that Christ is "living water for our bodies and souls," and the desire to provide affordable, low-maintenance water purification systems to people around the world. The Living Waters for the World committee also engages in health education and community development, and it is committed to having the water purification systems installed under local ownership in developing communities. Nine purifiers had been installed by December 2001, and between four and six were scheduled to be installed in 2002. The committee hopes to install twelve units a year in the future and welcomes other synods and presbyteries as partners in reaching this goal.

There are 796 churches and 126,505 members in the 12 presbyteries that make up the Synod of Living Waters. Louisville Presbyterian Theological Seminary is located within synod bounds; the synod also has a covenant relationship with Columbia Theological Seminary in Decatur, Georgia.

Scripture

"Peace I leave with you; my peace I give to you. I do not give to you as the world gives. Do not let your hearts be troubled, and do not let them be afraid" (John 14:27).

Let Us Join in Prayer for:

Synod Staff
Rev. David Snellgrove, executive
Elder Jane D. Hines, director, communication
Doreen Scott, administrative assistant
Stephen Hill, bookkeeper and editorial assistant

PC(USA) General Assembly Staff
Elder Joyce E. Evans, OGA
Daniel Fabia, BOP
Michael Fallon, Jr., BOP

Daily Lectionary
Ps. 66, 98, 116, 146
Isa. 30:18-26
Acts 2:36-41 (42-47); John 14:15-31

The Synod of Living Waters • 113

Let Us Join in Prayer for:

Elder Catherine P. "Kitty" Rasa, member, GAC

Presbytery Staff
Rev. Frank Jump, stated clerk
Steve Benz, executive presbyter
Rev. Lina R. Hart, associate executive presbyter
Rev. Michael V. Stanfield, associate executive presbyter
Rev. Spencer Parks, associate executive presbyter
Patty Dunlap, executive director for administration and treasurer
Mary Lawson, information/ events coordinator
Gwen Pyle, administrative/ financial assistant
Marian Hina Stuart, communications editor/hunger action enabler
Connie Umbach, resource center director/administrative assistant

PC(USA) General Assembly Staff
Bill Falvey, PPC
Steven Farkas, BOP

Daily Lectionary

Ps. 9, 99, 118, 147:1-11
Mic. 7:7-15
Acts 3:1-10; John 15:1-11

THE PRESBYTERY OF EAST TENNESSEE

B loom where you're planted." Fork Creek Presbyterian Church in East Tennessee is doing just that. It's planted almost equidistantly between the small towns named Loudon, Sweetwater, Madisonville, and Vonore. And its influence reaches beyond that imaginary square to take in as much of the world as it can handle.

More than 100 years old, Fork Creek has seen the placid agricultural nature of its land change to more aggressive farming, more industry, the development of lake recreation facilities, and the encroachment of interstate highways.

But people make a church. The people of Fork Creek have reached out to migrant Latin American farm workers, offering help to the workers and their wives and children in nearby trailer camps. In conjunction with St. Joseph the Worker Catholic Church in Madisonville, Fork Creek Presbyterian provided facilities, lunch, and a school bus to transport more than fifty children to the church for Bible school. Mothers accompanied the children and became acquainted with their new neighbors.

photo by Marian Stuart

Fork Creek Presbyterian Church in Sweetwater makes a difference in the world through its faith and concern.

An ongoing project is the making of colorful turbans. Women in this fifty-member church have made more than 850 turbans. One recipient wrote, "I wish to thank you for the turban I received from the Cancer Center in Monroeville, Pennsylvania. I didn't realize losing my hair would be as trying as it is. How thoughtful you are!"

The congregation of this rural church makes a real difference to the world through its faith and concern.

The presbytery has 80 churches with 15,977 members. Two Presbyterian-related colleges are within the presbytery's boundaries: Maryville College and Knoxville College. Service agencies include Bachman Academy, Sunset Gap Community Center, Newton Child Development Center, and the Morgan-Scott Project.

Scripture

Peter said, "I have no silver or gold, but what I have I give you; in the name of Jesus Christ of Nazareth, stand up and walk" (Acts 3:6).

HOLSTON PRESBYTERY

Tennessee

M agill Memorial Presbyterian Church is located in Roan Mountain, nestled along the banks of the Doe River and high in the Appalachian Mountains. The native stone building that houses Magill was completed in 1940, and the congregation has been a vital force in the community since then. In recent years the church faced dwindling membership and a graying congregation for more than a decade.

On January 7 and 8, 1997, a horrific flash flood struck the community, killing seven people and leaving hundreds homeless. Although the church was severely damaged, on the following Sunday morning the little congregation of twenty-five faithful members gathered as usual for worship. They prayed for strength and guidance, and then they began to clean up the mess and to minister to victims of the flood.

The devastating effects of the flood caused the church and the community as a whole to reevaluate their priorities. A wonderfully ecumenical spirit of cooperation developed. Magill provided leadership and labor, organizing relief efforts and securing funding. Ultimately twenty-four new homes were built and many others were repaired.

As Magill reached out in love into the community, the little church started to grow. In 1998 Magill began an outreach ministry that targeted children of unchurched families in the area. Now, on any given Wednesday night or Sunday morning, thirty-five or more children and youth are conspicuously and joyfully present at Magill, learning about and experiencing God's love in a very tangible way. They in turn have blessed the church with new energy and life.

The little church has grown steadily since the tragic flood of 1997. Magill called a stated supply pastor in 1999 and in May 2001 called a full-time pastor. In 2001 Magill received eighteen new members, which brought its total membership to seventy-six. Just as the spring floods bring new, fertile soil to the delta, producing abundant growth, so the flood brought new life to Magill through the enriching Spirit.

Magill is in Holston Presbytery, which has 68 churches with 9,303 members.

Scripture

And you shall know that I am the Lord, when I open your graves, and bring you up from your graves, O my people (Ezek. 37:13).

Let Us Join in Prayer for:

Presbytery Staff
Rev. Rich Fifield, executive presbyter
Paulette Thompson, office manager
Kim Hammond, finance manager
Susan Smith, director, resource center
Jim Kirkpatrick, director, youth and campus ministry
Chanda Reis, campus secretary
Craig Bell, director, Holston Camp
Patsy Laster-Ford, camp office manager
Peggy Crump, camp food services manager
Wayne Smith, camp building and maintenance manager

PC(USA) General Assembly Staff
Margaret Farmer, MSS
Rebecca Farnham, EDO

Daily Lectionary

Ps. 47, 68, 113, 147:12-20
Ezek. 37:1-14
Acts 3:11-26; John 15:12-27

Let Us Join in Prayer for:

Presbytery Staff
Sam Marshall, interim executive presbyter
Lucy Cummings, associate executive presbyter, outdoor ministries, recreation, and leadership
Patricia Taylor, associate, administration and finance
Audrey Anders, bookkeeper/secretary
Judith Wilson, resource center director
Rev. David Whiteley, director, Higher Education Ministries
Carmen Camburn, Pinecrest resident manager

PC(USA) General Assembly Staff
Rev. Maryann Farnsworth, FDN
Roxanna Farris, WMD
Arlene Fearon, BOP

Daily Lectionary
Ps. 49, 96, 138, 148
Dan. 12:1-4, 13
Acts 4:1-12; John 16:1-15

THE PRESBYTERY OF MEMPHIS

Tennessee, Arkansas, Missouri

The 12,500 members and 71 churches of the Presbytery of Memphis have supported the ministries of Pinecrest Conference and Retreat Center since purchasing the property in 1962. Its 450 acres lie west of LaGrange, Tennessee, a synodical college location and one known for its involvement in the Civil War. Armies used Pinecrest property for camping and strategic lookouts. This history, coupled with vast, undeveloped wooded areas, make Pinecrest a favorite retreat for groups and individuals.

During the summer, the ministries of Pinecrest speak to campers in a different way. Not only are they encouraged to enjoy, learn about, and care for our earth, but campers are also challenged to use God's gifts to learn more about themselves and their relationships with God and God's children.

A camper rappels at the Outdoor Challenge Camp.

The Outdoor Challenge Camp began seventeen years ago as a ministry of the Presbytery of Memphis. Twelve 11–13-year-olds travel to east Tennessee and North Carolina to rappel, whitewater raft, explore caves, hike, mountain bike, and kayak. Living in tents and battling the inevitable rainstorm, these kids push their comfort boundaries while backing off rock cliffs, swinging in trees, and heading down foaming water plumes. Counselors and directors who accompany these adventurers end up hearing about parental and sibling discord, school and personal conflicts, and doubts about God. Many a camper has entered The Outdoor Challenge as a child and returned as a young man or woman.

We are given life, precious and vulnerable, that we are called to develop in a variety of ways. The Presbytery of Memphis celebrates the gift of the earth, which sustains, challenges, and strengthens us so that we may use our lives to bring people to Christ.

Scripture
Sing to the Lord, bless [the Lord's] name; tell of [the Lord's] salvation from day to day (Ps. 96:2).

THE PRESBYTERY OF MID-KENTUCKY

Sixteen years ago, Highland Presbyterian Church and West Chestnut Street Baptist Church embarked on the Court Education Project. Highland is a predominantly white congregation on the eastern edge of downtown Louisville, and West Chestnut is a predominantly black congregation of the same size on the city's western edge.

Once each year, the two churches gather about a dozen members from each congregation in the district courtrooms of Jefferson County to watch court proceedings. Side by side they sit for one to three days, watching drug cases, traffic cases, violence cases, burglary cases, and warrant cases. They also pay an extended visit to the county jail, a place that has to be experienced to be understood. When the court visitation is complete, the groups gather for debriefing.

Two things emerge. First, a group of middle-class citizens gets an eye-opening look at a world that they know virtually nothing about. America's middle class typically does not appear in district court, and its members experience a stark revelation when they observe the participants and the proceedings.

But what is more important, when they look at exactly the same thing, black Americans and white Americans see very different things. White Americans expect justice in a courtroom, that right and wrong will usually be sorted out and that right will prevail, that a courtroom is fundamentally a place to be trusted. Black Americans' expectations are very different.

One of the most revealing questions that may be asked in the debriefing that follows is, "If you are driving down the street and a blue police light appears in your rearview mirror, signaling you to pull over, what do you expect will happen next, and how do you tell yourself to act?" White people and black people usually answer that question in entirely different ways.

The Court Education Project has become a powerful exercise in black-white communication, in seeing the world through someone else's eyes. Even after sixteen years, the project continues to thrive!

The Presbytery of Mid-Kentucky's 11,893 members serve in 54 churches. The presbytery also has 3 new church developments.

Let Us Join in Prayer for:

Presbytery Staff
Rev. Betty L. Meadows, general presbyter
Rev. Peggy Owens, associate general presbyter, education and mission
Nancy Pollock, assistant director, LARC
Mary Kutter, administrative assistant
Marcy Stein, secretary
Rev. Andrew Hartmans, director, Cedar Ridge Camp
Rev. Kenneth J. Hockenberry, stated clerk

PC(USA) General Assembly Staff
David Feder, BOP
Elder Ann Ferguson, PW

Scripture

"So you have pain now; but I will see you again, and your hearts will rejoice, and no one will take your joy from you" (John 16:22).

Daily Lectionary

Ps. 23, 92, 114, 149
Isa. 25:1-9
Acts 4:13-21 (22-31); John 16:16-33

Sunday Lectionary and Hymns

Acts 4:32–35
Behold the Goodness of Our Lord
PH 241

Ps. 133
Help Us Accept Each Other
PH 358; PPCS 137

1 John 1:1–2:2
Arise, Your Light Is Come!
PH 411

John 20:19–31
We Walk by Faith and Not by Sight
PH 399

THE LORD'S DAY

MINUTE FOR MISSION
RURAL LIFE EMPHASIS

The Acts of the Apostles remind us that the early Christians pooled their resources and no one among them was in need. Although that sounds like an unattainable ideal, people in rural areas pool their resources to support ministries that renew and revitalize community life.

In Wilcox County, Alabama, Trinity Church of Camden, Arlington Church of Annemanie, and a chapel are reaching out to youth in the area through tutorial and summer programs. Presbyterians in Green County, Kentucky, are leading efforts to revitalize their community, efforts that include a partnership with Highland Presbyterian Church in Louisville. Small business leaders from Louisville are sharing ways to launch new business ventures, and, at the same time, they are learning about rural Kentucky. The parish nurse program in Buffalo and Tower City, North Dakota, sponsored by Presbyterian, Lutheran, and Roman Catholic churches, is expanding its vision and offering a parenting skills program that includes spiritual development of parents.

Pooling the resources of church and community is essential to vital rural life and ministry. Grants for Rebuilding Rural Community Life from the General Assembly Council's Rural Ministry office have been part of a pool of resources that from 1992 through 2001 supported 136 rural communities in their revitalization efforts. More than 10 percent of the grants have supported ministries in racial ethnic communities.

Today people in rural communities and churches are being empowered by the same Spirit that Christ breathed on the disciples after the resurrection as he sent them back into the world in ministry and mission. Let us join in prayer, thanking God for sisters and brothers who proclaim the good news of the risen Christ as they live, work, and minister in rural communities across the church.

—*Elder Diana A. Stephen, associate for Small Church Networks*

Daily Lectionary

Ps. 93, 117, 136, 150
Isa. 43:8-13
1 Peter 2:2-10; John 14:1-7

Prayer

We thank you, gracious God, for the ministry of people in rural communities throughout your church who are working to revitalize church and community life. May your Spirit continue to empower them with new vision, energy, and creativity. May their vision be enlivened and community life rebuilt according to your way. In the name of the risen Christ, we pray. Amen.